AGENDA FOR ACTION

TOWARD PEACE
THROUGH DISENGAGEMENT

AGENDA
FOR ACTION

Toward Peace
Through Disengagement

JAMES P. WARBURG

ACADEMY BOOKS
Distributed by
MONDE PUBLISHERS, INC.
NEW YORK, N. Y.

AGENDA FOR ACTION
TOWARD PEACE THROUGH DISENGAGEMENT

For Joan
Jimmie, Jennifer and Philip
and
April, Andrea, Kay and
their children

CONTENTS

PREFACE

The period beginning with the Egyptian seizure of the Suez Canal, in July, 1956, has been one of kaleidoscopic change in the state of world affairs. For anyone deeply concerned with the dangers to American security which have arisen during this period as well as with the new opportunities which have unfolded, the recent past has been a period of intense study.

For every thinking person, it has been a period of acute anxiety—of wondering whether some way of escape might not be opened from the dangerously frozen positions of the cold war.

Escape obviously cannot lie in a continuation of the policies which have produced the present crisis.

The ideas presented in this book represent the author's effort to penetrate some of the urgent problems which have arisen and to develop a new approach to peace through gradual disengagement of the hostile forces confronting each other.

Many of the specific proposals advanced were first put forward for discussion in magazine and newspaper articles, in radio broadcasts and in lectures to a variety of audiences, during the winter and spring of 1956-1957. The resulting comment and criticism have enabled the writer to sharpen the specific proposals and, in some cases, to modify and improve them.

The focus of this study is upon the interlocked crises

in Europe and the Middle East and upon the opportunities presented by these crises for American initiative
in certain practical steps toward world disarmament and
economic development.

Since the Middle East may be *terra incognita* to a
considerable number of Americans, a brief sketch of
historical background has been provided in Chapter 3.

Acknowledgment is made to the editors of *The Reporter* for permitting the use of material which appeared
in several articles; and to *The Nation* for permitting the
extensive quotation in Chapter 5 from an article by Geoffrey Barraclough which appeared in its pages. The author
owes to Joseph Barnes a debt of gratitude for most helpful editorial criticism and to Ruth van den Bogaert for
her careful preparation of the manuscript.

JAMES P. WARBURG

Greenwich, Connecticut, May, 1957.

AGENDA FOR ACTION

TOWARD PEACE
THROUGH DISENGAGEMENT

THE TWIN CRISES

The crisis which began in 1956 is a twin crisis. It has affected both poles of power in what, a short time ago, looked like a bipolar world. The developments in Eastern Europe have profoundly shaken the foundations of Soviet power. The events in the Middle East have undermined the strength and solidarity of the anti-communist coalition.

For the moment, the European crisis and the Middle East crisis have offset each other. Russia would have found herself in much deeper trouble, had it not been for the blunders of the Western powers in the Middle East. The Western powers would be in an even more precarious position than they are today, had it not been for the Russian blunders which provoked the satellite revolt. The coincidence in time of the two crises has prevented either side from taking full advantage of the other's difficulties; it has also interlocked the solution of their respective problems.

Russia's problem in Eastern Europe is to find a way of withdrawing without loss of prestige or security from

3

a position which has, in the long run, become untenable.

The Western problem in the Middle East is to find a way of preventing the further intrusion of Soviet influence into an area from which Western retirement has become inevitable.

Neither problem can be solved without finding a solution to the other.

The solution of the European problem lies in negotiating a carefully phased withdrawal of Anglo-American and Soviet forces from that part of the Continent which lies west of the Soviet frontier, resulting eventually in the creation of a broad, militarily neutralized belt with a re-unified, neutralized Germany at its center. The first step in such a phased withdrawal might well be the evacuation of that part of Germany which lies between the Rhine and the Oder-Neisse rivers and the use of that neutralized area as a laboratory for the development of effective methods of inspection and enforcement.

The solution of the Middle East problem lies in negotiating with the Soviet Union a mutual hands-off agreement, with each side renouncing all hopes or ambitions to dominate all or part of the area. Such an agreement would include an arms embargo and a mutual covenant to aid the social and economic development of the Middle Eastern nations without either side seeking to gain, through such aid, political influence or economic advantage.

In other words, the twin long-range goals of American diplomacy should be the military neutralization of Europe between the English Channel and the Soviet border and the similar neutralization of the Middle East.

The attainment of these aims would necessitate changing the nature of NATO and of the Baghdad Pact. Likewise, it would necessitate changing the nature of the Warsaw Pact and of Soviet relations to Egypt and Syria. NATO would become, in effect, a unilateral declaration asserting that any Soviet incursion into the neutralized area, and particularly, any attack upon the nations of Western Europe, would be considered by the United States, Great Britain and Canada as an attack upon themselves. The Warsaw Pact would become a countervailing Soviet declaration that Russia would consider any Western incursion into the neutralized area as an attack upon herself. Similar countervailing declarations as to the Middle East would supplant the Baghdad Pact and the incipient Soviet alliances with Egypt and Syria.

In the Middle East as well as in Europe, the United Nations should be asked to endorse these hands-off agreements and to participate to the greatest extent possible in their enforcement, so that any violation by either side would instantly be recognized as a violation of the United Nations Charter calling for immediate action by the world organization.

What would be gained by the achievement of these twin aims?

The phased evacuation of Europe would separate the armed forces which now confront each other in central Germany, thus removing one of the most likely causes of war. It would relieve the neutralized nations of Europe of the burden of maintaining armaments and, more important, it would prevent the otherwise inevitable equipment of a number of European nations—especially Germany—with atomic weapons which they do not now possess. Thus, the phased evacuation of Anglo-American and Soviet troops would constitute a major step toward universal disarmament, while, at the same time, providing a gradually widening testing ground for the techniques of enforcement.

A hands-off agreement in the Middle East would have similar desirable consequences for all concerned. It would assure the United States that Russia would not get into a position to control or interfere with the production and transportation of Middle Eastern oil. It would assure the Soviet Union that the United States would not maintain or develop bases in the Middle East which would threaten Russia's vital centers. It would assure to the Middle Eastern countries the opportunity to develop their full independence and would leave it to them to fill the so-called vacuum created by British withdrawal.

In addition, since the hands-off agreement would include an arms embargo, the Middle Eastern countries would to all intents and purposes be demilitarized and thus would be relieved of the burden of maintaining military establishments. The extent to which this benefit would be realized would depend upon the extent to which the area could be internally pacified. This, in turn, would depend chiefly but not solely upon an Arab-Israeli peace settlement.

The dual proposition just stated represents a point of view which is contradictory to the American government's inflexible adherence to the frozen attitudes of the cold war. It derives from the belief that these attitudes are obsolete and irrelevant. This belief is now shared by a growing number of students of world affairs both here and abroad. It is shared by a considerable number of Democrats and quite a few Republicans in the United

States Congress, but reluctance to break party solidarity has so far prevented this bipartisan minority from forming an effective opposition to the cold-war policy inaugurated in 1948 and still supported by the bipartisan majority.

The writer has dissented from the cold-war policy since its inception. On April 5, 1948, just after the rape of Czechoslovakia, when President Truman had for the first time clearly set the course which the United States has followed ever since, the writer ventured to express, before the American Academy of Political and Social Science, a number of then most unfashionable doubts and misgivings.*

According to President Truman's explicit statement to the Congress on March 17, 1948, his then newly defined foreign policy rested upon the conviction that "one nation, and one nation alone" was responsible for the failure to make a just and lasting peace. In questioning this premise, the writer suggested that the Soviet Union had ruthlessly exploited rather than created the crisis in world affairs; that this crisis had arisen from a number of causes of which Soviet expansionism was only one; and that, if there had been no aggressive communist dictatorship in the world, we should still be confronted with the problems caused by the destruction and dislocation of a great war, by the Asian revolution, by the decline of European power, by the unexpected accretion of power to the United States and by the new dangers, new opportunities and newly aroused expectations created by the dawn of the atomic age.

* *Annals,* Volume 258, Philadelphia, 1948.

In adopting an oversimplified, scapegoat analysis of a complicated and many-sided world crisis, it seemed to this observer likely that our government might well become so preoccupied with the single aim of stopping Soviet expansion as to overlook the political, social, psychological and economic conditions which had actually made possible the spread of communism and the expansion of Soviet imperialism.

This danger loomed all the greater because our government appeared to be placing more and more reliance upon the military means of containment, in contrast to its earlier approach exemplified by the Marshall Plan. Such a shift in emphasis to rearmament and military alliances seemed likely to commit the United States more and more to the preservation of the *status-quo* and to undermine American influence upon the masses of mankind seeking such changes as land reform, the establishment of better living conditions or emancipation from foreign domination.

A final critical observation, made at a time when the United States still held a monopoly of atomic weapons, was to the effect that our government had apparently not yet grasped the single, most important fact of the atomic age; namely, that war had ceased to be even a last-resort instrument for restoring peace and justice.

Summing up this evaluation of our then new foreign policy, the writer stated the belief that it would logically lead either to a war in which victory would be indistinguishable from defeat, or to a fatal alliance between Soviet communism and most of the revolutionary forces at work in the world, especially in China and the rest of

Asia. (China had then not yet succumbed to communist dictatorship.)

As an alternative to excessive preoccupation with military containment, the writer ventured to suggest that the United States should pursue two broad aims:

1. That the United States should throw its great moral and economic strength behind the emerging, non-communist, progressive movements throughout the world, respecting the native characteristics of those movements, whether or not they conformed to the particular political and economic prejudices and predilections of the American people.

2. That the United States should throw the full weight of its military and economic resources behind the United Nations, with the openly avowed purpose of strengthening that organization to the point where it could reliably enforce universal national disarmament.

The paper concluded with the following observation: "If these were our positive aims and if we pursued them with intelligence and determination, a large part of our present limited and negative objective would automatically be realized. We should then draw to our side those existing forces which can and will, if supported, stop communism and which can and will achieve One World. We should, in other words, achieve the stopping of communism as the by-product of a positive policy."

The passage of time has, year by year, strengthened the convictions then expressed. Their application to the twin crises now existing in Europe and the Middle East is set forth in the following chapters. The discussion begins with the European crisis, because in Europe lies the key which can unlock the frozen positions held throughout the past decade.

The proposition advanced as to Europe is one which the writer has advocated, *mutatis mutandis,* ever since the winter of 1948-1949. It now no longer represents merely the view of an inconsequential minority. At the Summit Conference of July, 1955, Prime Minister Sir Anthony Eden put forward a proposal which represented a start along this line. In 1957, the Soviet government suggested that this Eden proposal should be taken up again. On May 8, 1957, James Reston of the *New York Times* asked President Eisenhower at his press conference what he thought of the suggestion. The President's reply, though vague, indicated that there might be in the making some change in the hitherto inflexible attitude of the American government. The President said that any proposal to establish a demilitarized zone would have to be examined "with respect to the vital character or the critical character of the areas affected, and consequently even a small one is very difficult to get initiated." However, the President expressed the belief that mutual inspection would ultimately come about "through some such evolutionary development" and that any proposal in that direction that seemed fair to both sides would be "sympathetically entertained and earnestly studied."

This statement was far from indicating that the President recognized the need for a wholly new approach to the problem of Europe based upon phased disengagement, but it showed that the Chief Executive was not unaware of the rising tide of opinion favoring such a course.

In Europe, a number of important leaders had expressed serious interest in such an approach, among them the leaders of the opposition parties in Great Britain and Germany. Hugh Gaitskell, head of the British Labour Party, had explored the possibilities in a series of lectures at Harvard University.* Erich Ollenhauer, leader of the German Social Democrats, had recently visited the United States and had left no doubt that he would make a revision of NATO policy a major issue in the elections to be held in the Federal Republic in September.

In this country, George F. Kennan, former United States Ambassador to Moscow, had expressed himself to a Congressional committee as favoring a revision of NATO policy. Chester Bowles, our former Ambassador to India had returned from a visit to Moscow in February, 1957, convinced that the phased neutralization of Europe should be seriously explored.**

The chief obstacles remained Chancellor Adenauer's intransigent adherence to a bankrupt policy and his powerful influence upon the American government.

Anyone who read the European press could not fail to be aware of the growing realization that the costly maintenance of conventional forces, even if armed with atomic weapons, would provide no security against invasion; and that, on the contrary, the atomic armament

* Godkin Lectures, published under the title *The Challenge of Coexistence,* Harvard University Press, 1957.
** *New York Times Sunday Magazine,* May 12, 1957.

of the NATO forces on the Continent would be more likely to provoke than to prevent a war in the course of which all of Europe would be devastated.

The alternative to present NATO policy is neither appeasement nor surrender. The alternative is cautiously phased disengagement and withdrawal through give-and-take negotiation of self-enforcing agreements.

TWO

OUR SECOND CHANCE

IN EUROPE

If the objective of United States postwar policy in Europe has been to reach a peace settlement, it must be admitted that the policy pursued has brought such a settlement no nearer than it was at the conclusion of World War II.

With the single exception of the brilliant interlude which included the sponsorship and execution of the Marshall Plan, American policy in Europe has, in fact, been a dismal failure. To say this is not to belittle occasional successful improvizations, such as the intervention in Greece and Turkey and the Berlin Airlift. Nor does this negative evaluation imply that the overall failure of American policy in Europe has been exclusively due to mistakes made in Washington. The British, French and Germans have contributed their share of blunders; and the whole problem of reaching a European peace settlement has, of course, been distorted by the ruthlessly selfish and intransigently uncooperative policy of the Soviet Union.

13

I

Evolution of United States Policy in Europe

In appraising American postwar policy in Europe, it is necessary to recognize that a large part of its failure has been due to decisions made prior to World War II and to developments during that conflict. Russia's intrusion into Eastern Europe had its origin in the Western Powers' policy of appeasement, which surrendered the heart of Europe to Hitler, and in a strategic concept of coalition war against Hitler which permitted the Russian armies to overrun all of Nazi Germany's eastern empire and even a part of Germany itself. Given the betrayal of Eastern Europe into Hitler's hands and Hitler's attack upon Russia, it was probably inevitable that the coalition's conduct of the war would follow substantially this course. In any case, that is what happened.

At Yalta, an attempt was made to regain by diplomacy what had been lost through appeasement and through the subsequent course of the war. The mistake was not to attempt such a venture. The mistake was to assume its success. This assumption, and an altogether too rosy view of Soviet intentions, led to the premature demobilization which stripped Western diplomacy of any backing of physical power, save only that of the atomic bomb.

Thus, American postwar diplomacy began with two strikes against it: the first being Russia's physical possession of Eastern Europe; and the second the absence of physical power due to the unwarranted belief that Yalta had assured the restoration of East European freedom.

From this inauspicious beginning, our postwar policy

in Europe has stumbled through a succession of failures into a dead-end street, from which, until October, 1956, there seemed no escape.

There would be no point in analyzing how we got into such a position, were it not for the fact that recent developments within the Soviet orbit have provided us with a wholly unearned second chance to get out of it.

The assertion that our European policy has been a failure rests upon the validity of the following thesis:

1. There can be no peace in the world without a European settlement.

2. There can be no European settlement so long as Germany remains partitioned.

3. Neither Russia nor the Western powers are strong enough to gain control of a united Germany, or weak enough to yield such control to the other.

Conclusion: The only viable policy is one which aims at the reunification of Germany on terms which will insure its freedom and independence, while at the same time providing the maximum assurance that a united German nation will never again become a pawn, partner or primemover in aggression against either its eastern or western neighbors.

Originally, this was substantially our government's view. The thesis was, in fact, fundamental to the Potsdam Agreement of 1945. But so many mistakes were made prior to and in this agreement that it never became operable. And, when the bankruptcy of the Potsdam Agreement became apparent, our government abandoned the basic concept, with disastrous results. It now moved toward the opposite thesis—that a united Germany could and should be incorporated in the anti-communist West. The evolution is worth tracing.

The Potsdam Agreement was stultified by certain prior wartime commitments and by the incorporation of vestigial remnants of certain abortive notions developed in Washington during the war.

The annexations of East German territory, foreshadowed at Yalta and executed at Potsdam, were in flagrant violation of the principles of a just peace and in contravention of the specific pledges embodied in the Atlantic Charter. Moreover, the Russo-Polish land-grab in the East aroused French annexationist desires in the West; and, when these desires were frustrated, caused the French to obstruct the basic concept of the Potsdam plan for the four-power government of a truncated Germany as a single political and economic entity.

Elements of the truly nonsensical Morgenthau Plan for the de-industrialization of Germany crept into the Potsdam Agreement and stood in flat contradiction to the amputation from Germany of its most productive agricultural provinces.

The concept of unconditional surrender meant the assumption by the victors of full responsibility for the future of Germany.

Worst of all, the four occupying powers set out to impose what amounted to a social, political and economic revolution upon Germany, without having agreed among each other as to what sort of a new Germany they wished to create.

A year after its signature, the Potsdam Plan was a

shambles. The four zones had become separate satrapies, hermetically sealed off from each other. Russia was milking the German cow at one end, while the United States and Britain were forced to feed it hay at the other. After a careful, on-the-spot study, this observer, then a war correspondent, submitted a plan for the revision of the Potsdam Agreement and the restoration of four-power government of Germany as a single entity. Although favorably regarded by our authorities in Germany and by the German experts in the State Department, the plan failed to gain the approval of Secretary of State, James F. Byrnes.*

In the following year, Secretary of State Marshall made the first serious attempt to grapple with the German problem. Unfortunately, the ill-fated Moscow Conference of April, 1947, was held under the unfavorable auspices of the newly-declared Truman Doctrine, and, chiefly for this reason, ended in complete failure. It was not so much the actual intervention in Greece and Turkey as the accompanying declaration of belligerent global policy that ended whatever chances there may have been to reach an understanding with regard to Germany, and made Moscow unable to understand and appreciate the subsequent, truly generous offer of the Marshall Plan.

The Moscow fiasco and the rejection by Russia of the Marshall offer turned the incipient cold war into a grim reality. From here on, each side became increasingly the prisoner of its own propaganda and of the domestic climate of opinion which it created. From here on, Europe was definitely divided into two hostile orbits with

* See Author's *Germany—Bridge or Battleground*, pp. 354-359; Harcourt Brace, 1947.

the line of cleavage running through the heart of Germany.

There now developed in American policy a fateful trend toward the creation of a West German state. It was wholly logical to undertake an economic merger of the Western zones and to incorporate them in the Marshall Plan, but one did not have to be a soothsayer to predict that the creation of a separate political entity would lead to a Russian attempt to drive the Western powers out of Berlin and to the creation of an East German Soviet satellite, thus freezing Germany's partition.*

The Kremlin's first major move in this new situation was to consolidate the Iron Curtain frontier by eliminating the Czechoslovak salient. This was accomplished by the communist coup in February, 1948, a move which outraged and alarmed the West and brought about a new phase in the cold war.

After the rape of Czechoslovakia, the overall emphasis in American policy shifted from the wisely conceived philosophy of the Marshall Plan toward the ill-conceived notion of military containment—from trying, through generous economic aid, to make Western Europe immune to communist subversion, toward an attempt to secure Western Europe against physical invasion by rearmament. This shift in emphasis gave additional impetus to the idea of making West Germany into a soverign state. Again, it required no prophetic gift to foresee and to warn that, if any part of Germany were to be protected against invasion from the East, logic would sooner or

* See Author's *Put Yourself in Marshall's Place,* page 37; Simon & Schuster, 1948.

later demand that the Germans be rearmed in order to participate in their own defense.*

The North Atlantic Treaty

Throughout the winter of 1948-1949, it was known that a treaty of alliance was being negotiated between the United States, Canada and certain of the nations of Western Europe. Beyond the fact that the treaty would commit the United States and Canada to consider an attack upon the European signatories as an attack upon themselves, little was known of its content. Reports from Europe clearly indicated, however, that some of our proposed allies, notably France, were demanding more than a promise that the United States would go to war with an aggressor. They wanted a guarantee against invasion, not merely the promise of another liberation. "Next time you liberate us," said the French premier, Queuille, "you will be liberating a corpse."

This European demand was wholly understandable, but loaded with dynamite. To accede to the request would mean that the United States would commit itself to hold off a Soviet invasion in central Germany or, at the very least, at the Rhine.

In a series of memoranda to the newly-appointed Secretary of State, Dean Acheson, and to the committees of Congress, this observer ventured to point out the disastrous consequences which would flow from such a commitment. These memoranda did not criticize the basic declaration of American solidarity with the nations of

* See Author's *Rearming Germany—How Stupid Can We Be?*, Current Affairs Press, 1949.

Western Europe.* The memoranda did, however, point out the disadvantages of a multilateral treaty, as against a unilateral declaration of solidarity, especially if such a treaty were to divert Western Europe from recovery to rearmament, and even more if it were to commit the United States to a defense of the West European frontiers. As an alternative to the proposed treaty, the following course of action was suggested:

An Alternative Proposed (February, 1949**)

1. That the United States and Canada should unilaterally declare that they would consider any attack upon Western Europe as an attack upon themselves;

2. That the United States should endeavor to negotiate, instead of a North Atlantic Alliance, a tripartite Treaty of Europe under which the United States, Great Britain and the Soviet Union would guarantee the security of all the European nations between the Atlantic seaboard and the Soviet frontier. It was suggested that this tripartite guarantee be given on two conditions; namely, that the nations so guaranteed would agree to maintain only such military establishments as might be necessary to maintain internal order; and that they would agree to permit inspection by United Nations authorities of all military establishments and all factories capable of manufacturing offensive weapons;

* As a matter of fact, the writer had publicly advocated precisely such a declaration ten years earlier, in March, 1939, as the only way of preventing Hitler from launching World War II. See his *Our War and Our Peace*, Chapter 4, Farrar and Rinehart, 1941.

** See Author's *Last Call For Common Sense*, pp. 202-229; Harcourt Brace, 1949.

It was further proposed that the Treaty of Europe should provide for the withdrawal from the Continent west of the Soviet frontier of all American, British and Soviet armed forces, except that the Western powers combined and the Soviet Union should each be entitled to maintain in Germany and Austria the equivalent of not more than one armored and one motorized infantry division, until the German and Austrian peace treaties should have been signed.

Among the arguments put forward for this alternative were these contentions: that it would save the cost of re-arming Western Europe and avoid interrupting its economic recovery; that it would hasten the attainment of Western Europe's economic self-support and political stability, thus strengthening its defense against the primary threat of communist penetration; that it would get the Russian army out of Eastern Europe, while still leaving a mutual trip-wire against aggression; and that it would enable the United States, Great Britain and Canada to preserve their freedom of action and to build up their military power where it would count most heavily as a strategic reserve in the event of war.

This alternative was never seriously considered. It is stated here in detail because, after eight years, it has again become relevant.

The Fateful Stretching of the Commitment

Shortly after the North Atlantic Treaty had been signed and its text published, this observer was asked to testify for or against its ratification before the Senate Foreign Relations Committee. The statement prepared for the Committee favored the basic declaration of solidarity, although it pointed out certain dangerous geographic loopholes which might lead to miscalculation by a would-be aggressor. On the other hand, a warning was sounded against the possibility that the treaty might be stretched into a commitment, such as the French desired, to fight an invader at the West European frontier. It was contended that the United States should not commit itself in advance to any given strategy in the event of war.*

The testimony of this witness further brought out that a promise to defend Western Europe at the Elbe, or even at the Rhine, might well turn out to be an unfulfillable undertaking; and that the promise would almost certainly be unfulfillable unless we were prepared to station in Europe more or less permanently a sizeable American force and, in addition, to rearm the Germans. It was pointed out that the Russians could scarcely be expected to sit still on their side of the Iron Curtain while a force capable of holding their own army at bay was being built up across the line of demarcation—especially if that force were to include a resurrected German army. Furthermore, the opinion was expressed that rearming all or any part of Germany would frighten and alienate all the recent victims of Nazi aggression and would be particularly injurious to the morale of France.

The senior Republican on the Committee, the late Senator Arthur Vandenberg of Michigan, stated emphatically that no such stretching of the commitment was contemplated. Chairman Tom Connally (D), of Texas, concurred. Various Senators referred to Secretary Acheson's specific promise that no additional American troops would be sent abroad and to his flat repudiation of the

* *Congressional Record,* May 10, 1949.

idea that the United States would ever acquiesce in the remilitarization of Germany. Moreover, the Senators pointed out that administration witnesses had denied that Western Europe would be diverted from recovery to rearmament; that it was not intended greatly to increase the West European forces but merely to reequip and modernize the existing 12 West European divisions.

In reply, this witness permitted himself the observation that, if these plans were to be carried out, it should be made clear to the Europeans that NATO would not provide a shield against invasion but merely a deterrent to armed aggression. The Senators agreed that all doubt on this score should be removed, and their decision was so reported in front-page newspaper stories on the following day.*

Strangely enough, within a few months of the treaty's ratification, the United States assumed precisely the commitment which the Senate had explicitly rejected. Within a short time, a powerful American force was sent to Germany; and, no sooner was this done, than the outcry was heard:

"Why should our boys defend the Germans? Why shouldn't they help to defend themselves?"

Korea merely provided the excuse for the openly declared decision to rearm West Germany—a decision which had become inevitable, once the United States had slipped into the commitment to defend Western Europe at the line of the Iron Curtain.

How and why the United States slipped into that commitment is a story which remains untold even today, but the consequences are clear.

* E.g., *New York Times,* May 11, 1949.

By 1952, it had become evident that, if NATO was actually to become a shield against invasion, its Mediterranean flank would have to be protected through the inclusion of Greece and Turkey. This was accomplished at the Lisbon Conference and a goal was set for a total NATO force of some 90 divisions, of which about 60 were to guard Western Europe. 12 divisions were to be supplied by West Germany.

Two years later when these Lisbon goals had proved unattainable, the fateful decision was reached to offset a deficiency of manpower by equipping the defense forces with so-called tactical atomic weapons. Thus equipped, it was thought that 30 divisions could provide a shield for Western Europe.

But even the 30 divisions never materialized. Whereas, in 1949, Western Europe had 12 divisions available for NATO, in February 1957, Western Europe was providing less than 6 divisions for its own defense.* Apart from 5 American and 4 British divisions, there were available to NATO: 1 Canadian-Danish division, 3 undermanned Belgian divisions, 1 Dutch division and 1 French training division, the rest of the French army being in North Africa. As for the Mediterranean flank, it had all but disintegrated, due chiefly to the Anglo-Greek-Turkish quarrel over Cyprus.

Six years after the United States had demanded West German rearmament, there was not a single German division in the field; but the decision to remilitarize Germany had shaken the morale of Western Europe, exacerbated East-West tensions and left a partitioned Germany ticking like a time-bomb in the heart of the European

* London *Economist*, February 23, 1957.

Continent. This threat to peace could hardly be expected to diminish when a streamlined, professional German army, equipped with atomic weapons would finally take the field.

What had this painful 8-year effort to build a shield accomplished? Could anyone believe that the pitifully small NATO forces, even if fully equipped with atomic weapons, could do anything more than bravely fight a brief delaying action? Could anyone believe that much would be left of Western Europe after that delaying action had been fought?

The simple fact which our government had all along refused to recognize was that, after the overhasty demobilization at the conclusion of World War II, there never has been a way to make Western Europe safe against Russian invasion, except by preventing that invasion from being attempted.

The Russian threat to Western Europe never was a threat of military conquest. The Russian threat was and to a certain extent still is a threat of political subversion —a threat which has been greatly reduced by the restoration of Western Europe's economic health and political stability through Marshall Plan aid. But, even if one assumes that the intention to invade did at some time exist, the fact remains that it was never executed, either before NATO came into existence or later, when French involvement in colonial wars and German delay in rearming created the most inviting opportunities. If the intention existed, the deterrent was provided not by the wholly inadequate conventional forces in Western Europe but by the certain knowledge that an attack upon an almost defenseless Western Europe would bring on

World War III, with the United States ranged against the Soviet Union. The Russians know that in such a war there could be no such thing as victory. They are also only too well aware that their purposes are better served by continuing to fish in the troubled waters of an uneasy peace.

There was one possible explanation for the fateful American decision, in 1949, to undertake the erection of a shield against the invasion of Western Europe; namely, to bolster European morale and to create the will to resist. If such was, indeed, the reason for the undertaking, its purpose was defeated by the psychological effect of the decision to rearm Germany.

The Unused Bargaining Counter

This ill-advised decision did, however, have one unforeseen virtue. It created a bargaining counter. Between September, 1950, when the United States demanded West German rearmament, and May, 1952, when the European Defense Community Treaty providing for German contingents was signed, the Russians made a number of overtures which, if explored, might have led to an all-German settlement. These overtures indicated that the reunification of Germany on terms acceptable to the West might be had at the price of the abandonment of German rearmament and of German participation in the NATO alliance.

The American government and the West German government of Chancellor Adenauer were, however, unwilling to bargain. They were by now determined to include not only West Germany but all of Germany in NATO and not to negotiate a German settlement until they could

do so from what they called "a position of strength,"—
meaning, until they had actually created a West German
army of half a million men. The delusion that Russia
could thus be compelled to permit all of Germany to
become a NATO partner persisted for the remaining
years of the Truman administration.

When General Eisenhower was elected President, having previously served as NATO commander, it seemed
reasonable to hope that his administration would re-
examine a policy which, far from creating a position of
strength, was rapidly producing a situation of dangerous
weakness. Hopefully, this observer submitted a paper to
the President-elect shortly before his inauguration, first
analyzing the German deadlock and the rapidly deteri-
orating morale of Western Europe and then outlining in
detail a plan for negotiating an all-German settlement
based upon both sides giving up their intransigent
positions.*

Unhappily, the new administration took over—lock,
stock and barrel—the bankrupt European policy of its
predecessor. For four years, it continued to insist upon
the creation of a German army which neither the French
nor a great many Germans wanted. For four years, it
continued to demand that a reunited Germany must have
the right to join NATO—which was tantamount to demanding unconditional surrender on the part of the
Kremlin. And, for four years, the Kremlin refused free
elections—that was the Soviet bargaining counter—demanding in one way or another that the East German
communist apparatus should have a dominant voice in a

* See Author's *Germany—Key to Peace,* pp. 251-326; Harvard
University Press, 1953.

new all-German government. This was equivalent to demanding unconditional surrender on the part of the West.

Meanwhile, European opinion was split wide open over the question of German rearmament. The parliamentary ratifications of the E.D.C. Treaty were delayed from month to month. More than a year elapsed before even Chancellor Adenauer could obtain the consent of a reluctant *Bundestag.* It was August, 1954, before the French Assembly finally rejected the treaty signed in 1952. Even though a substitute method of bringing West Germany into NATO was soon devised, the rejection of the E.D.C. Treaty killed, for the time being, all hope for the political and economic union of the countries of Western Europe; and, with this hope, vanished most of the enthusiasm for "Europeanism" that had existed in Germany. There remained only a military coalition.

The strange fact which now emerged clearly was that West Germany, though still unarmed, had already become the indispensable keystone of the NATO structure.

Between 1954 and 1956, it became evident to most thinking Germans that reunification and partnership in NATO were mutually exclusive. The signs were more and more unmistakable that, if the Germans did not soon obtain reunification through a settlement negotiated between Russia and the West, they would before long make their own deal with the Kremlin, on terms not necessarily consistent with Western interests.

This was the dead-end street into which our wrongheaded and inflexible policy had taken us.

The revolt of two major Soviet satellites in the autumn of 1956 suddenly and dramatically opened up a possible exit from this dangerous, frozen position.

II
Developments in Eastern Europe

From 1946 to 1956, Soviet leadership, having obtained military control over Eastern Europe, sought to impose a more or less uniform pattern upon a region whose chief characteristic was and is its lack of uniformity. Some of the East European nations had come into being only after the break-up of the Turkish Empire; others had been created even later, after the dismemberment of Austria-Hungary at the conclusion of World War I. Bulgaria, Rumania, Albania and parts of Yugoslavia and Hungary still bear the imprint of centuries of Turkish domination. Poland and Czechoslovakia bear the marks of alternating Slavic and Western conquests.

Broadly speaking, the northwestern part of the region, comprising East Germany, Poland and Czechoslovakia and most of Hungary, belongs culturally to the West, while the southeastern portion leans more toward a Slavic affiliation. The northwestern group is Roman Catholic or Protestant; the southeastern group is predominantly Greek Orthodox or Moslem. Most of the area employs the Latin alphabet but the Cyrillic alphabet is still used in Bulgaria and Yugoslavia.

Some of the countries—Bulgaria, Hungary, Rumania and Yugoslavia—are predominantly agricultural. Czechoslovakia is a modern industrialized state; Poland is rapidly becoming one. Social conditions vary greatly in the agricultural areas, with feudal latifundia traditionally existing in Hungary, Poland, East Germany and Rumania, while the land in Czechoslovakia, Bulgaria and

Yugoslavia has long been more widely distributed among peasant holders.

The democratic tradition was strongest in Czechoslovakia and East Germany. In Poland and Hungary, parliamentary democracy had for long periods been submerged by authoritarian rule. In the southeastern area, except in parts of Yugoslavia, the peoples had very little experience of democracy prior to World War II.

When the Russian armies "liberated" Eastern Europe from Nazi conquest, Soviet leadership sought at first to install "friendly" governments, but this term soon developed a far more extensive meaning. The definition of a "friendly" government not only came to mean a government subservient to Moscow but a communist dictatorship patterned after the Soviet design. It is obvious that the imposition of collectivized agriculture and forced industrialization under communist, police-state dictatorships, with the leadership taking its orders from Moscow, would encounter various kinds and varying degrees of resistance in a highly diversified area.

Czechoslovakia, with the strongest Western cultural ties and the strongest democratic tradition, managed to remain outside the satellite orbit until February, 1948. Even as a satellite, it has maintained the highest living standard in the region.

Yugoslavia was the first to revolt, in the same year in which Czechoslovakia was subjugated. Yugoslavia was able to revolt partly because it was not directly contiguous to the Soviet Union and because it had liberated itself instead of being "liberated" by the Red Army; but primarily because it alone had a leader strong enough to stand up to Josef Stalin. Tito's revolt was not against communism but against Soviet domination. Although primarily nationalist in nature, the Yugoslav rebellion had profound ideological implications which later manifested themselves in the doctrine that there is "more than one road to socialism."

Tito's break-away and his willingness to take Western aid and even to enter a Balkan alliance with Greece and Turkey was a profound shock to the Soviet system. An infuriated Stalin took drastic measures to see that nothing similar might occur in any of the other satellites. Leaders suspected of Titoist tendencies were liquidated and, in general, the reins of Soviet control were tightened. In the long run, these measures only served to strengthen the suppressed spirit of resistance; but, so long as Stalin lived, the smoldering fires were kept under control.

During the Truman administration, the United States had, on the whole, maintained a quiescent attitude toward Eastern Europe, except as to Yugoslavia. With respect to the latter country it had pursued a wise policy of giving aid without pressing Marshall Tito to join the anti-communist alliance. During the election campaign of 1952, John Foster Dulles and General Eisenhower talked about a new "policy of liberation" but, when this apparently belligerent talk frightened Western Europe, General Eisenhower rapidly abandoned the idea. Once in office, the Eisenhower administration in effect continued the quiescent policy of its predecessor.

Stalin's death, in March 1953, the liquidation of Lavrenti Beria and the relaxation of controls by Georgi Malenkov marked the beginning of a serious satellite revolt. The East German uprisings of July, 1953, provided the first outward evidence of rebellion directed not so much against Soviet domination as against the harsh terms of existence imposed by the local, Moscow-dominated communist regime. The Western Powers did nothing to encourage the revolt. Malenkov's fall, the suppression of the uprisings and a partial return to rigid controls then kept matters outwardly quiet for another two years, when a very similar uprising occurred in the Polish city of Poznan. Simultaneously, Czech workers in Pilsen demonstrated against a communist-imposed currency reform. Then again, there was quiet—but only for a short time.

What really set off the fireworks was the de-Stalinization program launched by the now famous secret speech of Nikita Khrushchev at the 20th congress of the Soviet Communist Party in February, 1956. The denigration of the demi-god, who had for more than 30 years ruled with a rod of iron, and the sudden destruction of the myth of his infallibility shook not only the structure of the satellite empire but the very foundation of the dictatorship in Russia itself. Overnight, the unchallengable dogmas of Stalinism were thrown open to challenge. The quasi-religious faith of the communists themselves in the infallibility of their regime was shaken. Small wonder, then, that this wholly unforeseen development should have a profound impact upon the satellite peoples.

The Polish and Hungarian revolts of October, 1956, for the first time combined resentment against indigenous communist rule with nationalist rebellion against Russian domination. For the first time in ten years, the prestige of

Soviet leadership no longer commanded blind obedience within the Communist Party. Beneath the surface of nationalist revolt there was an uprising, if not against communism as such, then at least against those particular brands of communist dictatorship under which the peoples of Poland and Hungary had suffered.

In Poland, the revolt was staged by a government responsive to popular sentiment and, hence, no longer willing to take orders from Moscow. In Hungary, the people revolted against a government obstinately subservient to Moscow. In Poland, the Russians were forced to seek a compromise; they could not use force without risking the outbreak of a full-scale war. In Hungary, the Russians could and did resort to brutal force, because the government asked for help in maintaining itself in power against the will of its own people.

The significant fact in both countries was that the rebellion was spear-headed by what might almost be called a new type of middle class—not the traditional capitalist bourgeoisie seeking political power to protect its propertied interests, but a new, largely propertyless and distinctly socialist-minded intelligentsia—an intelligentsia which included not only students, scholars and writers but soldiers, factory workers and peasants as well. The revolt of this intelligentsia was not against socialism but against the mismanagement of socialism by the communist dictatorship. It was a revolt against bad planning, inefficient administration, inflexible adherence to Stalinist dogma and the suppression of dissent.

Ironically enough, this new, revolutionary element had been created by communist inspired and directed mass education, by the training of scientists and by the propagation of a managerial elite in a supposedly egalitarian, proletarian society. The spread of literacy and scientific knowledge had undermined, probably beyond repair, the foundation of mass ignorance and mass acquiescence in leadership decisions upon which the "dictatorship of the proletariat" had been founded. It appeared that, while the Kremlin might not yet have dug its own grave, it had certainly bought itself a plot in the cemetery.

The ultimate outcome of this startling and wholly unexpected development was unpredictable. No one could tell how far, if at all, the revolt might spread. Bulgaria, Rumania and Albania appeared to be very little affected and, for the time being at least, there were few signs of disaffection in Czechoslovakia. The latter was, no doubt, surprising to anyone not familiar at first hand with the stubborn but non-violent nature of the Czechoslovak people.

Inured to a thousand years of foreign domination, the Czechs acquired a habit of passive resistance not conducive to open revolt. The hatred of communism is probably more deep-seated in Czechoslovakia than in Poland, but, whereas the Poles hate and have every reason to hate the Russians, the Czechs, since the betrayal of Munich, are ambivalent as between Russia and the West. Moreover, the Czechs under communism have suffered less than the other satellite peoples from Soviet exploitation and local communist mismanagement. It is quite possible that, if living conditions in Czechoslovakia should change for the worse as the result of the Polish and Hungarian revolutions, popular sentiment will swing violently against a continuation of the present satellite relationship.

It is more than probable that such a development may

take place. The economic monolith of the Soviet empire has been destroyed. In the foreseeable future, Poland and Hungary will be economic liabilities for the Soviet planners. Two results of the October revolutions are fairly certain: *First;* the Kremlin will no longer be able to deal with the satellites as a bloc; it will have to deal with each satellite separately. *Second;* the intra-satellite economic relations will be radically altered.

East Germany and Czechoslovakia, the two most industrially developed satellites, are heavily dependent upon Polish coal. It seems almost certain that the Gomulka regime will seek to retain more of its coal output at home than it was permitted to keep under Moscow direction. Should this be the case, the East German and Czechoslovak industries will either have to cut down their production or turn elsewhere for coal supplies. Russia is in no position to export coal in large quantities. If these two satellites turn to the West, there is a distinct danger of friction with Moscow. If, on the other hand, production is cut back in East Germany and Czechoslovakia, there will be unemployment and political unrest.

The various political and economic forces set into motion by the events of October, 1956, will certainly lead to further developments not only in the satellite countries but within the Soviet Union itself. The Soviet regime may mellow or resort to renewed repressive measures. It may develop new relationships with the countries of Eastern Europe or seek to re-impose the old relationships. The latter course seems almost certain in time to provoke further revolt and, should that revolt spread to East Germany, might well endanger the peace of the entire world.

III
Our Unearned Second Chance

One thing is unequivocally clear: the events of 1956 within the Soviet orbit presented the West with a radically altered situation as to the future of Europe. Poland and Hungary were no longer armed outposts of Soviet power threatening Western Europe. They had suddenly and dramatically become areas of resistance to Soviet power dangerous to leave in the rear of any westward Soviet move. The satellite armies as a whole had become undependable, especially so in the crucial northwestern area.

The Soviet note of November 17, 1956, to the Western powers showed that the Kremlin was acutely aware of this altered situation. The Soviet proposal for a mutual withdrawal of Russian and Anglo-American troops from Europe, while unacceptable in the form presented, showed that the Kremlin might now be ready to seek a face-saving device by means of which it might withdraw its coercive power from positions which had become ultimately untenable.

Our government failed lamentably to seize the opportunity thus unexpectedly presented. The Soviet proposal was brushed off as insincere propaganda and no counterproposal was made to explore its sincerity. In part, this was no doubt due to Western preoccupation with the crisis which had simultaneously erupted in the Middle East. But that was not the whole story. The cold warriors in Washington, who had not wanted to negotiate a European settlement until they had a formidable bargaining position, now counseled against negotiation because

Russia's unsuspected weakness in Eastern Europe had suddenly been exposed.

The great moment, when Western initiative might well have prevented the return of Soviet tanks to Budapest and facilitated the beginning of a Soviet withdrawal, was lost.

On December 7, 1956, this deeply concerned citizen wrote once more to President Eisenhower, expressing the opinion that, while the revolution in the Soviet orbit had increased the danger of a major war, especially if the satellite rebellion should spread to East Germany, it had also presented the United States with its greatest opportunity to move forward toward a European peace settlement.

It was suggested in this letter that the United States might reply to the Soviet proposal substantially as follows:

The necessity for NATO was created by the stationing of Soviet forces in Eastern Europe and the creation of Soviet controlled satellite armies.

If the Soviet Union is now prepared to begin a withdrawal of its own forces from Eastern Europe and to grant the East European countries an increasing measure of independence, the United States will welcome such action and do everything in its power to encourage and facilitate it, giving due consideration to the interests of Soviet security. Specifically:

1. The United States will respect the independence of the East European countries and will in no way try to influence their political or economic development or to loosen such political and economic bonds as they may voluntarily wish to maintain with the Soviet Union.

Should any of these countries request economic assistance and should the United States be willing to comply
with such requests, any such aid will be given without
any political conditions.

2. The United States is willing to consider favorably
the Soviet proposal for a mutual withdrawal of troops
from Europe. Such withdrawal can, however, be accomplished only by a step-wise procedure.

As a first step the United States is prepared to
recommend to its Allies a withdrawal of Anglo-French-
American forces to the West bank of the Rhine, provided that Soviet forces are withdrawn to the East
bank of the Oder and the Western Neisse rivers, with
suitable arrangements for aerial and ground inspection
and adequate provision for the maintenance of the
status quo in Berlin pending the reunification of
Germany.

The United States is further prepared to recommend
to its Allies an agreement with the Soviet Union
whereby the Federal Republic of Germany would be
released from NATO and the German Democratic
Republic would be released from the Warsaw Pact.
Thus the ground would be prepared for the reunification of Germany as a nation without military commitments to East or West, with its neutrality guaranteed by
both the Soviet Union and the Western powers.

It would be the hope of the United States that the
first step, above outlined, could be followed by further
steps leading to a general security agreement for all of

Europe lying between the Soviet borders and the Atlantic Seaboard, ultimately involving the withdrawal from this area of all Soviet, American and British forces.

Should this hope be realized, the NATO alliance will ultimately be reduced to a simple declaration by the United States that it would regard any attack upon the countries of Western Europe as an attack upon itself, while the Warsaw Alliance would be reduced to a similar declaration by the Soviet Union that it would consider any attack upon the countries of Eastern Europe as an attack upon itself.*

The reader will not have failed to recognize the striking similarity between this proposal and that put forward eight years earlier, before NATO came into being. Events had now swung full circle, leaving the United States standing substantially where it stood in the winter of 1948-1949.

The simple truth of the matter is that NATO in its present form is not only obsolete but that it is rapidly losing its value as a bargaining counter. The NATO structure is based upon strategic conceptions irrelevant to the postwar distribution of power and to the changed nature of physical power in the atomic age. The sole element in NATO which is still valid today is the basic declaration of solidarity between the American and European parts of the Atlantic Community.

The United States must continue to recognize that it

* This proposal was endorsed in substance by the Arden House Disarmament Conference held December 14-17, 1956, and was personally taken to President Eisenhower by three of its participants: Senators Flanders (R) of Vermont, Sparkman (D) of Alabama, and Congressman Brooks Hays (D) of Arkansas.

has a vital interest in Europe's cultural and political freedom, in its economic health, and in its achievement of a difficult readjustment to the loss of colonial empires. But the way to restore health and vitality to the European part of the Atlantic Community is to heal, rather than to fortify the cleavages which now split Europe asunder.

The way to defend Europe's freedom is to help its peoples to unite their strength and to become a major factor in making the Atlantic Community the source of dynamic support for inevitable change, rather than the last citadel of an outmoded and dying world order.

The political and economic unification of Europe, so auspiciously begun with the establishment of a European Coal and Steel Community under the Schuman Plan of 1950, was aborted by the efforts to create a "European Army." In 1957, the dream was revived by the treaties aiming at the establishment of a common market but, so far, the dream has been only that of a Little Europe—a Western Europe which, even if united, would not be a viable entity, especially if weighed down by the burden of armaments.

Europe cannot be reunited unless it is demilitarized. A demilitarized united Europe can become a far stronger barrier to Soviet expansion than an armed West European Union.

What better way is there to heal the cleavage which now divides the European family of nations than the military neutralization of all of its members, relieving them of the burden of maintaining armaments, freeing them from the presence of foreign troops and leaving them at liberty to determine their own political and economic future?

What better way is there to move toward the ultimate abolition of war through universal disarmament than to create an area in which the techniques of reliable enforcement may be tried out?

The European policy which we have been pursuing leads, if not to war, to indefinite continuation of a precariously maintained balance of terror. The longer the world continues in this state, the greater will be the advantage of the totalitarian dictatorships over the democracies. Not only can the dictatorships more easily sustain the ever-increasing burdens of maintaining both atomic striking power and conventional forces; but also, by their very nature, they enjoy a freedom of maneuver denied to the democracies by their inherently slow processes of policy formation. It is far more clearly to the American interest than to that of Russia to end the existing state of affairs.

The second chance to revise our European policy, created for us by the satellite revolt, will not last forever. Given time, the Kremlin will bend every effort to restore its position in Eastern Europe. Meanwhile, if we fail to seize the opportunity of the moment and continue along our present course, it is not hard to see what will happen. The British will reduce their forces stationed on the Continent. The French will remain bogged down in North Africa. Germany, now at long last seriously at work to create an army, will definitely become the dominant power in Western Europe. This will mean that, eventually, the fate of Europe will be decided, not by the United States, Britain and France in negotiation with the Soviet Union, but by Russia and Germany.

What is more, unless the United States takes the initiative in Europe, it is unlikely that it will find a solution to the problems of the Middle East. A hands-off agreement in the Middle East requires the West to withdraw from actually held positions of advantage; it requires the Soviet Union to give up little more than its hopes and ambitions in that area. The *quid pro quo* for Western withdrawal from the Middle East positions which threaten Soviet security is Russian withdrawal from positions in Eastern Europe which threaten Western security.

Thus, failure to seize upon our second chance in Europe imperils not only the future of that Continent but the future of the vital crossroads which link Europe to Africa and Asia.

Brief Chronology of United States Policy in Europe

1945

February 12	The Yalta Agreement
August 2	The Potsdam Agreement
	The demobilization and redeployment of U.S. Forces. Cancellation of Lend-Lease.

1946

	Breakdown of the Potsdam Agreement.
	Europe in trouble. Loan to Britain.
March 5	Churchill foreshadows Truman Doctrine at Fulton, Missouri.

1947

March 12	The Truman Doctrine. Intervention in Greece and Turkey.

March-April	The Moscow Conference.
June 5	Marshall at Harvard announces Marshall Plan for European Recovery.
July 2	Molotov walks out of Marshall Plan.
October 5	Russia announces Cominform.
December	Congress gets proposals for interim aid to Europe and 4-year European Recovery Program totalling $17 billion.

1948

February 17	Communist Coup in Czechoslovakia.
March 17	Brussels Treaty—Defense Pact between Britain, France and the Low Countries.
June 2	London Agreement to merge three Western zones of Germany. Soviet protest and demand for 4-Power Conference. When protest is ignored, Russians start Blockade of Berlin.
June 11	Vandenberg Resolution authorizes U.S. to join defense pacts under Article 51 of U.N. Charter.
June 28	Berlin Airlift begins.

1949

April-July	Congressional debate over North Atlantic Treaty and Military Aid Bill.
May 10	Berlin Blockade lifted.
August 14	Federal Republic of Germany elects its first government with Konrad Adenauer as Chancellor.

| October 7 | After protesting formation of West German state, Moscow creates German Democratic Republic in Soviet Zone. |

1950

March 16	Churchill demands "German contribution" to Western defense.
May 10	French Foreign Minister Robert Schuman proposes coal and steel merger for France, West Germany, Italy, Holland, Belgium, Luxembourg and Great Britain. Britain declines.
June	Outbreak of Korean War distracts attention from European problems.
September 12	Acheson proposes drastic increase in European rearmament and inclusion of German contingents in NATO defense force.
October 18	Soviet protest and counter-proposal for unification of demilitarized Germany.
December	French, in desperation, propose "Pleven Plan" for "European Army."

1951

| January | General Eisenhower, as NATO Commander, visits Europe and recommends going slowly on German rearmament. His testimony induces Congress to authorize sending 4 additional American divisions to Germany. |

March-June	After extensive exchange of notes between Russia and the Western Powers, Deputy Foreign Ministers meet in Paris in fruitless attempt to arrange agenda for 4-Power Conference on Germany.
	Adenauer exploits German trading position to alter "Pleven Plan."

1952

February 19	At London Conference, apparent agreement reached between French and Germans with Germans getting most of their demands. German contribution fixed at 12 divisions and 1,700 tactical aircraft.
February 25	At Lisbon Conference, Turkey and Greece admitted to NATO and force goals are set which later prove unattainable.
March 10	Soviet note puts forward detailed proposal for all-German settlement. Rejected on March 25.
April 9	Additional Soviet proposal. Likewise rejected, but strong sentiment in favor of 4-Power Conference develops in Europe. This is ignored by Washington.
May 26	Contractual Agreements restoring full sovereignty to Bonn government signed in German capital.

May 28	EDC Treaty signed at Paris.
	For the remainder of the year, U.S. is preoccupied with election campaign, during which Dulles sends up trial balloon on a new "policy of liberation." Revolt against EDC Treaty spreads throughout Europe.

1953

January	Eisenhower administration takes office and, to all intents and purposes, adopts the European policy of its predecessor.
March	Stalin's death and Malenkov's softer policy further slow European action toward ratification of EDC treaty.
June-July	East German uprising.
October 26	Moscow proposes 4-Power Conference.
December 5	Italians and Yugoslavs agree to withdraw from Trieste.
December 8	Bermuda Conference (U.S., Britain and France) agrees to 4-Power Conference and reaffirms NATO as foundation of Western policy.
December 14	Dulles threatens "agonizing reappraisal" of U.S. policy unless EDC ratified.

1954

| January 25 to | Berlin 4-Power Conference. Molotov |

February 13	proposes General Security Agreement. Western Powers blame Soviet Union for failure.
June 5	Greece, Turkey and Yugoslavia sign military alliance.
August 30	French Assembly rejects EDC Treaty.
October 3	Substitute plan for bringing West Germany into NATO adopted at London.
December 2	Moscow threatens to form anti-NATO alliance.
December 21	Dulles declares NATO forces will use tactical atomic weapons to defeat an invasion.

1955

February 8	Malenkov resigns, replaced by Bulganin and Khrushchev.
March 21	Moscow announces Warsaw Pact (treaty signed with satellites May 14).
May 15	Austrian Peace Treaty finally agreed to.
May 26	Soviet leaders go to Belgrade to patch up relations with Yugoslavia.
July 18-23	"Summit" Meeting at Geneva. Eisenhower proposes aerial inspection. Eden Plan rejected.
September 15	Adenauer goes to Moscow. Fails to make progress toward German unification.
November 10-16	Foreign Ministers' Meeting at Geneva achieves nothing.

1956

April 18	Moscow announces dissolution of Cominform.
May 6	NATO Council appoints committee of 3 to recommend ways of strengthening organization.
October 22	Trouble starts in Poland and Hungary.
October 30	Moscow declares willingness to "examine" question of stationing its troops in satellites.
November 10	U.S. rejects Swiss call for Summit meeting.
November 17	Soviet Note proposes mutual withdrawal from Europe. Rejected by U.S.

1957

During the first months of 1957, the Soviet Union put forward a number of feelers, repeating in substance the proposal of November 17, 1956, and specifically suggesting that the Eden Plan be reconsidered. In February, Khrushchev told Chester Bowles that these moves were seriously meant. On May 8, President Eisenhower gave a somewhat vague indication that some sort of disengagement might be considered.

THREE

HISTORICAL BACKGROUND SKETCH
OF THE MIDDLE EAST

NOTE: This chapter is not essential for the reader who is in a hurry to grapple with the problems of the present, nor will it add to the information of those familiar with Middle East history. It has been included for those who may find it useful to have, as background to the chapters which follow, at least a cursory survey of the historical development of an area which has only recently assumed prominence in contemporary developments.

The term, Middle East, is loosely applied to an area reaching from India to the eastern shore of the Mediterranean. For the purposes of this discussion, it should also include Arab North Africa, though not the non-Arab lands lying to the south. Pakistan, though Moslem and a member of the Baghdad Pact, belongs to Asia rather than to the Middle East, especially since its eastern portion is separated from West Pakistan by some thousand miles of Indian territory.

The three areas with which we are concerned are:
1) The Fertile Crescent, stretching from Mesopotamia
to the Nile; 2) Iran and Turkey, the non-Arab flanks of
the Crescent; and 3) The Arab countries of North Africa.

I

The Fertile Crescent

The heart of the Middle East lies in Egypt and Asia
Minor. Here, in what is now the center of the Moslem
world, lie the earliest sources of what we call "Western"
civilization.

Out of ancient Palestine came the concept of the infinite value and perfectibility of the human individual—a
concept which is the foundation-stone of Western democracy. Here were born the three great monotheistic religions: Judaism, Christianity and Islam. The ancient
Egyptians gave us the calendar. The Sumerians of Mesopotamia—now Iraq—first divided the circle into degrees
and the day into hours and minutes. The Babylonians
invented the wheel and the Egyptians contributed the
lever and the screw. It was here, in Mesopotamia and in
Egypt, that the first ox-drawn plow and the first systems
of irrigation enabled man to produce more food than he
could eat and thus led to the earliest known division of
labor.

For the past century this once prosperous region has
been so much of a low pressure area on the weather map
of the world that one tends to forget its past millenia of
ascendancy. Egypt has existed for seven thousand years.
During that time, eleven civilizations have risen and fallen
in Mesopotamia. It is estimated that in ancient times

20,000,000 to 25,000,000 people prospered on the fertile alluvial soil of the Tigris and Euphrates valleys, where today some 4-5 million inhabitants of modern Iraq live in conditions of poverty, disease and ignorance. The present population of Jordan is estimated to be only two-fifths of what it was under Roman rule.

Two thousand years ago, the area now occupied by Syria, Lebanon, Israel and Egypt represented the economically most advanced portion of the Roman empire. In fact, the industrial relations of East and West were then the reverse of what they are today; the Orient exchanged its manufactured products for the raw materials of the western countries. The "fine linen of Beth Shaan" is mentioned in the Talmud. The word "gauze" is derived from Gaza where dyed silks and cottons were manufactured. The Emperor Diocletian fixed a maximum price for the textile products of Beisan, then called Scythopolis. There are ruins of densely populated cities in the Tigris and Euphrates valleys, from Aqaba to Gaza and in many other parts of Asia Minor where wars, deforestation, soil erosion and the silting up of canals have reduced the Garden of Eden to a desert inhabited by nomads.

The decay of urban life and of agriculture in Asia Minor began with the first Arab conquest of the area in the seventh century A.D., continued through the period of the crusades and the second Arab invasion, and reached its low point in the four hundred years of Turkish rule from 1517 to 1918. Under the Turkish system of selling the privilege of collecting taxes to the highest bidders among the rich families, who, in turn, farmed out the privilege to lesser agents, the population was unmercifully exploited. One of the most pernicious features of this system of taxation was the imposition of a tax on every tree and vine, which accounts in large measure for the deforestation. Farmers who had for centuries carefully cultivated terraced soil or irrigated land were reduced to growing and living on the coarsest foods. Many became nomads, whose goats devoured the remaining vegetation. Canals and irrigation systems silted up. Terrace walls crumbled. Cities were abandoned. The population decreased and the remaining inhabitants became to all intents and purposes the slaves of the few rich land-owning or money-lending *effendis*.

While the earliest records of human civilization have been found at both ends of the Fertile Crescent, it is probable that the early Sumerians or Babylonians and the Egyptians had no contact. Later, as each pushed along the bow of the Crescent, the two civilizations came into contact and into intermittent conflict in what is now Syria, the Lebanon and Israel.

Whereas the history of Mesopotamia is one of a continuous rise and fall of successive civilizations, from about 4000 B.C. until the time of the Persian conquest, the history of Egypt, despite repeated invasion and occupation, is more or less continuous. This is because, from the earliest times, Egypt was able to absorb its conquerors, often being strongly influenced by them but never wholly destroyed.

The "Old Empire" of Egypt (about 4000 to 2700 B.C.) with its capital at Memphis in the Nile delta, constituted what was probably the earliest known nation-state. The kings, or Pharaohs, of this period built the great pyramids at Gizeh and the Sphinx.

The "Middle Empire" (2700 to 1670 B.C.) had its

capital at Thebes and afterward at Tanis, both in the upper part of the Nile valley. During this so-called Feudal Period, Egypt reached a high degree of prosperity. Great reservoirs and irrigation canals were constructed to carry the waters of the Nile beyond the boundaries of its annual overflow. Handicrafts flourished and a rich culture found expression not only in architecture but in painting and remarkably fine sculpture. Paper, ink and the art of writing were developed, first in hieroglyphs and then in a phonetic language. By this time, Egypt had also become the foremost maritime trading nation, sending its ships out into the Red Sea and along the coast of the Mediterranean.

Toward the end of the Middle Empire, Egypt was for the first time conquered by invaders from the North. A tribe known as the Hyksos descended from Asia Minor and established the dynasty of the Shepherd Kings.

The Egyptian, Thutmose III, who reigned from 1501 to 1447 B.C., was the first great general in history. He not only drove out the invaders but conquered most of Asia Minor and part of the Sudan. His war-fleets ranged as far north as the islands in the Aegean Sea. Thutmose III, often called "the Napoleon of Egypt," welded an empire which lasted until the Persian conquest almost a thousand years later. This "New Empire" marked the height of Egyptian power.

After the Persians in the sixth century B.C., came the Greeks; and, after the Greeks, the Romans. From each, Egypt absorbed new cultural wealth. Alexandria became one of the cultural centers of the Mediterranean world. After the fall of Rome, the Arab tide flowed over Egypt in the seventh century A.D., bringing with it not only

Islam but the Arab language. And, finally, in the 16th century, there came the Turks, under whose rule Egypt languished for almost four hundred years.

Unlike Asia Minor under Arab-Turkish rule, Egypt was not depopulated. Blessed with the annual flooding of the Nile waters, Egypt was not nearly so dependent upon flood control and irrigation nor so vulnerable to deforestation as Mesopotamia. Today, Egypt's problem, unlike that of the Arab countries at the other end of the Fertile Crescent, is one of overpopulation. Out of 22,000,000 inhabitants, some 20,000,000 are miserably poor peasants.

Due to the nature of its long history, the Egyptian ruling class has a psychological problem somewhat different from that of the Arab peoples of Asia Minor. The Arabs conquered Asia Minor and left but few vestiges of previous civilizations; then they, in turn, were conquered by the Turks. But the Arabs kept their own language, their religion and their tribal and race consciousness. The Egyptians, on the other hand, absorbed not only a part of their culture but important segments of their racial background from successive waves of invaders. They adopted the religion and, in a modified form, the language of their Arab conquerors. The upper crust of present-day Egyptian society is of mixed racial origin. The resulting absence of a true sense of "Egyptianness," despite Egypt's long history as a nation, has produced a sensitive insecurity which readily turns into chip-on-the-shoulder aggressiveness. This is important to understand, if one seeks to comprehend contemporary developments.

While present-day Arab nationalism manifests similar characteristics, it has somewhat different origins, due to a different course of development at the eastern end of the Fertile Crescent.

Whereas the Egyptians had layer after layer of different civilizations imposed upon them, the Arabs imposed their civilization upon a large part of the world in a spectacular conquest which took place within three generations. The penetration of Syria and Mesopotamia by Arab desert tribes began several centuries before Mohammed, but the true Arab conquest began in the 7th century A.D., when the Moslem faith energized the Arab movement. The cultural evolution thus set in train consisted of two processes—Islamization and Arabization. These two forces worked hand in hand but did not stop at the same frontiers. The Moslem faith spread farther than the Arab conquest and remained in some conquered countries even after the Arab tide had receded. The area permanently Arabized consisted of Asia Minor (except Anatolia), Egypt and North Africa. Here, in addition to adoption of the Moslem faith, Arabic became the mother tongue and the native populations absorbed a preponderant admixture of Arab blood.

The high tide of the Arab conquest reached into Spain and southern France, and eastward as far as Turkestan. The ebb set in with the conquest of Persia by the Ottoman Turk, Selim I, in 1515, followed by the Turkish overrunning of Iraq, Syria, and Egypt. Under Suleiman the Magnificent, the Turkish dominion was extended from Algeria to the Persian Gulf. For the next three centuries the Arab world was submerged under Turkish rule, yet, when the Turkish tide in turn receded, the conquerors had left remarkably little imprint upon the conquered.

The first Arab revolt was staged by an Albanian Turk and frustrated by an Englishman. Mehemed Ali was sent from Albania by the Sultan of Turkey to fight with the British against Napoleon Bonaparte in Egypt. After Napoleon's defeat and withdrawal, (1801), Mehemed Ali remained in Egypt, destroyed the power of the Mameluke Beys and made himself Pasha. Calling upon the Arabs to revolt, he first conquered the Arabian peninsula and Syria and then built a navy and fought a naval war against the Greeks. In 1820, he conquered part of the Sudan. Had it not been for European intervention, Mehemed Ali would have established a second Arab empire under Egyptian leadership.

France at this time favored the Egyptian rebellion because its success would threaten Britain's life-line through the Middle East. For the same reason, Lord Palmerston wished to suppress the rebellion and to have Egypt remain under loose Turkish control. Under Palmerston's leadership, Anglo-Russian intervention destroyed Mehemed Ali's naval power and, in 1841, the Concert of European Powers imposed a settlement depriving Mehemed Ali of most of his conquests. Mehemed's son, Ibrahim, remained for a time in Syria but was then forced to withdraw. Mehemed Ali himself was conceded the title of hereditary Viceroy of Egypt, under Turkish suzerainty.

Ibrahim's temporary rule in Syria had one effect of lasting importance. It opened Syria to Western missionaries. The spread of Christianity by these missions was less significant than the fact that they opened schools and re-awakened the Arabs' pride in their own language.

In the 1850's Anglo-French rivalry for control of

Egypt reached a second acute stage when the French engineer, Ferdinand de Lesseps, obtained a concession from Khedive authorizing his company to construct the Suez Canal. Confirmation of this concession was blocked for several years by Palmerston's influence at Constantinople, but eventually the canal was completed in 1869. Six years later, Disraeli acquired for the British government what amounted to a controlling interest in the Canal Company by buying out the holdings of the bankrupt Egyptian government. In 1879, an Anglo-French dual control was established over Egypt's finances. When this failed to assure payment of Egypt's debts and aroused rebellious sentiments, the British moved in with military force. Thus began, in 1882, a British occupation which, though announced as temporary, was to last for three-quarters of a century.

Anglo-French rivalry in Egypt continued until 1904, when Germany's rise as an ambitious, would-be colonial power brought about the *Entente Cordiale*. This Anglo-French agreement gave Britain a free hand in Egypt and France a free hand in Morocco and Tunisia. This ended French political interference but French cultural influence in Egypt remained strong. Even today, French—not English—is the second language of Egypt.

In 1914, after Turkey joined the Central Powers in World War I, Britain declared Egypt a British protectorate. In 1918, the Arab countries of Asia Minor were liberated from Turkish rule. (The circumstances surrounding Arab liberation will be discussed in Chapter Four because of their profound influence upon the contemporary crisis.)

The imposition of wartime controls and the liberation

of the Arab countries aroused a strong nationalist movement in Egypt. In 1922, the British abolished the formal
protectorate but continued the occupation. Resentment
mounted and, in 1936, the British signed a treaty with
Egypt agreeing to terminate their occupation by 1956,
meanwhile limiting their garrisons to Cairo, Alexandria
and the Canal Zone.

During World War II, Suez served the British as a base
for the entire Middle East area, thus adding to the Egyptians' resentful sense of being a part of the British Empire
rather than an independent nation. Egyptian non-belliger-
ence, even when Egypt itself was menaced by Axis invasion, was a significant product of accumulated anti-
British sentiment. A further important cause of Egyptian
resentment was British imperialist policy in the Sudan
which Egypt considered historically a part of her
territory.

II
The Non-Arab Flanks—Iran

To the East of what was once the Fertile Crescent lies
Iran and, to the northwest, Turkey. Both are non-Arab
members of the Islamic family.

About 4,000 years ago the Aryans, an Indo-European
people, coming from somewhere in the West and North—
possibly from what is now south-central Russia—split
into two parts, one moving into India and the other into
Iran. (Iran means "Land of the Aryans.") The two main
groups settling in Iran were the Medes and Persians.

Under the leadership of Cyrus the Great (580-530
B.C.) the Persians first conquered the Medes and then,
within the span of a single generation, established an

empire reaching from the Mediterranean to the Punjab and from the Nile to central Asia.

The Persians were tolerant of conquered peoples, giving a considerable amount of autonomy to the local satraps whom they installed as representatives of the Great King. Yet they had a strong sense of a civilizing mission, building roads, irrigation systems and canals. Darius I (521-485 B.C.) completed the first canal linking the mouth of the Nile to the Red Sea.

In the 4th century B.C., this great Achaemenid Persian empire began to decay, mostly through provincial revolts in which Greek mercenaries played an increasing part. In 331 B.C. Alexander the Great, having subjugated the quarreling Greek city-states, conquered the Persian Empire. Eight years later, after Alexander's premature death, his empire fell apart. Seleucus, one of Alexander's generals, established himself as King of Persia and the succeeding Seleucid dynasty ruled Iran until it succumbed to another Aryan invasion from the North, this time by the Parthians.

In spite of more or less continual wars with Rome, the Parthians lasted until about 224 B.C., when a new Persian dynasty, the Sassanids, established themselves in power. Under Artaxerxes I and his successors, the struggle with Rome assumed the aspects of a religious war between Zoroastrianism and Christianity. The Sassanian period, which lasted for over 4 centuries, is regarded by modern Iranians as a Golden Age, second only to the first great Achaemenid period.

In the 6th century A.D. Turkish tribes began to press upon both Persia and the Roman Empire at Byzantium, sometimes allying themselves with the Persians against

Rome and at other times siding with the Romans. In 641 A.D., when both sides had exhausted themselves, the Arabs swept in to conquer Persia.

Under the Moslem Caliphs, Persia became a part of Islam but it never became Arabic. Unlike other peoples overrun by the Arab Moslems, the Persians retained their own language and culture. In fact, while adopting the religion of their conquerors, the Persians modified it to suit themselves, forming the Shiite Moslem sect which later spread eastward and even into parts of the Arabian peninsula.

Religious and political differences gradually disintegrated the eastern part of the Islamic world. By the latter part of the 10th century, there were two kingdoms in Persia, the Samanids in the East and the Buwayhids in the West. Under the Samanids, there was again a revival of ancient Persian culture. This, however, was cut short by successive Turkish and Mongol invasions which lasted from about 1,000 to 1500.

Tamerlane, a Central Asian Turk, was the last of these dreaded invaders. His withdrawal marked what is generally considered the beginning of modern Persia, or Iran. The new Azerbajanian Safavid dynasty established the Shiite faith as the state religion, and made the military force an instrument of the Crown. Henceforth the Shah was both king and saint.

During the next two centuries, the Persians were under constant pressure from the Ottoman Turks, who had conquered Constantinople in 1453 and were likewise beginning to press upon the Arab world to the South.

At the beginning of the 18th century, Russia began to compete with the Turks for influence over Iran. In 1722

Peter the Great seized the southern and western shores of the Caspian Sea. Although this conquest was later yielded, Russia, by about 1800, had established something like a protectorate over the weak Qajar dynasty.

It was now the turn of Britain and France to enter the Persian arena. Napoleon briefly eyed Persia as the gateway to India, an idea later to be cherished by William II of Germany. But the chief struggle for influence in the 19th century was between Russia and Great Britain. Each obtained concessions from the Shahs only to be elbowed out by the other.

In 1906, Persia underwent a revolution against the absolute monarchy. A parliament, the *Majlis,* was created and a constitution was reluctantly granted by the Shah, who promptly violated it and called in Russian troops to aid in suppressing the subsequent rebellion.

A year later, Russia and Great Britain, alarmed by the rising influence of the Kaiser's Germany, reached an agreement which set up a Russian sphere of influence in northern Iran and a British sphere in the South. The Persians were bitterly resentful but powerless to prevent this dual occupation.

World War I brought both the Turks and the Germans temporarily into Iran. After the defeat of the Central Powers, Lord Curzon obtained an outrageous agreement from the Shah which, if consummated, would have placed Iran completely under British domination. Even though the *Majlis* repudiated the agreement, the episode left a lasting hatred of the British.

One reason for the determined British interest in Iran was that oil had been discovered there in 1908. The concession for exploration had been obtained by the Anglo-

Persian Oil Company, originally a private concern but later controlled and largely owned by the British government.

Iran's population is a conglomerate of ethnic groups, many of them speaking different languages, centering around a Persian core. The Persians have a fierce pride in their country and in their past. The Shah is the symbol of their strength—the strength which they demand of a leader. Cutting across this traditional, authoritarian pattern is the conflict between the peasant village and the city—the conflict between the land-and-village-owning elite, of which the Shah is the head, and the urban intellectuals whose demands for reform the present Shah supports. Recent material improvements have done little to change the social climate. Iran is impatient for development, yet reluctant to make decisions; anxious for assistance, yet resentful of advice; distrustful of Russia and resentful against Britain. Iranian relations with the United States are on the whole friendly, but American association with British oil interests, since 1954, may endanger this relationship.

Turkey

Turkey, the northwestern, non-Arab flank guardian of the Middle East, presents a curious anomaly. On the one hand, it is the sole remnant of the regressive wave of conquest which, under Selim I and Suleiman the Magnificent, submerged Asia Minor, North Africa and a large part of southeastern Europe. On the other hand, modern Turkey is, except for Israel, the most advanced nation in the Middle Eastern area.

The great Ottoman Empire established by Suleiman

lasted intact for over a century and a half. After Europe recovered from the ravages of the Thirty Years War (1618-1648), the Turks met their first major defeat at Vienna in 1683. This marked the beginning of a slow retreat from Europe which was not completed until the first decade of the 20th century. Chiefly because of its interest in Egypt, Britain became the dominant influence over a slowly decaying Sultanate throughout the 19th century. This influence lasted until Britain seized Cyprus from the Turks in 1878 and occupied Egypt in 1882. Prior to this time, the Turks had already lost their hold on North Africa, but the Arab countries of Asia Minor remained firmly under Turkish control until they were liberated by the British during World War I.

Originally, the Allies (Britain, Russia and France) had planned the almost complete dismemberment of the Ottoman Empire. The Treaty of Sèvres (1920) would have carried out this design, had not the Bolshevik revolution and the Turkish revolution intervened. The Bolsheviks renounced Tsarist claims and France ultimately withdrew from a temporary occupation of southwestern Anatolia.

As the result of defeat and humiliation, the Sultanate was overthrown and a republic established in 1923 by Mustapha Kemal Pasha, the strong man of modern Turkey, who assumed the title, Atatürk. The capital was moved from its vulnerable site at polyglot Istanbul to the interior at Ankara and, under the firm, authoritarian rule of Kemal, an extraordinary modernization took place. The alphabet was Latinized. Women were emancipated. The Turkish people, freed from both the corrupt oppression of the Sultanate and from the shackles of Islamic

orthodoxy, rapidly regained their self-respect and
awakened to a new pride in their nationhood.

Modern Turkey, even more than present-day Iran,
nurtures an abiding hatred of Russia. Unlike the Iranians,
the Turks have to a large extent forgotten their hostility
toward Britain, although it has been somewhat revived
by the contemporary dispute over Cyprus. The Turks do
not share the violent Arab hostility toward Israel.

The Turkish army is by far the strongest in the Middle
East. Numerically, it is larger than that of any European
member of the NATO alliance. Tough-minded and physically hardy, the Turks are the only real bulwark against
Soviet invasion in the Middle East.

III
The Maghreb

It remains now to trace briefly the history of the North
African Arab West—in Arabic, the *Maghreb*.

Most of the North African littoral was first settled by
the Phoenicians, whose capital city was Carthage in what
is now Tunisia. After the destruction of Carthage in 146
B.C. at the conclusion of the long Punic Wars, the
southern shore of the Mediterranean remained under
Roman rule until the Vandals sacked the Eternal City and
for a time established themselves in parts of North Africa.
In 534, most of the area was restored to the rule of the
Roman Byzantine Empire until the Arab invasions in the
7th and 8th centuries. Thereafter, Islam replaced Chris-
tianity in most of North Africa. In the 12th century the
Almohade Empire stretched from Morocco to the Nile.
In the 16th century, the Turks gradually conquered the
Arab empire, gaining control of most of North Africa,

after a century-long struggle with the Catholic rulers of Spain and Austria. Throughout more than three hundred years of Turkish overlordship, Arabic remained the common language in most of the area.

During the late 18th and early 19th centuries, the pirates of the Barbary Coast whose main strongholds were in Algeria, Tunisia and Tripoli (now Libya), harrassed Mediterranean shipping. The young United States Navy put an end to their depredations upon American commerce in the wars of 1805 and 1815. The Dey of Algiers continued, however, to prey upon European trade until, in 1830, Marechal de Bourmont, Minister of War for Charles X of France, sailed with 350 ships and 37,000 soldiers to capture the Algerian capital and begin a century of French occupation.

During the reigns of Louis Philippe and Napoleon III, sporadic resistance continued. French colonization on a major scale set in under the Third Republic. The organized settlement of European immigrants was accompanied by the building of roads, harbor installations and agricultural development, all undertaken in the belief that these activities would result in an "assimilation" of the native Arabs and Kabyles which would transform them into contented and useful second-class Frenchmen. This colonial rule, organized under the fiction of granting the Algerian native population the rights of French citizenship, lasted for 84 years, surviving two world wars without any major rebellion.

Tunisia fell under French influence during the latter half of the 19th century. The Husseinite Dynasty had striven, since 1705, to assert its autonomy under Turkish rule. A succession of Beys succeeded in instituting a number of reforms but incurred such heavy indebtedness to France and Italy that an International Control Commission was appointed in 1869. Italian rivalry for control of Tunisia incited France to intervene and to conclude with the Bey of Tunisia the Bardo Treaty of 1881, under which Tunisia became a French protectorate. French colonization and exploitation, similar to that which took place in Algeria, dates from this period. The Tunisian nationalist reaction did not set in until about 1920, after the first World War.

Morocco was the last of the North African countries to come under European domination. Never fully conquered by the Turks, the Sherifian Empire of Morocco had long been an independent nation when the United States achieved its independence. One of George Washington's first official communications as President was addressed to the "Emperor of Morocco." European rivalry for African colonies brought on a collision of interests in Morocco, resulting first in the Anglo-French *Entente* of 1904 and then in the settlement of Algeciras in 1911. The latter agreement, mediated between France and Germany by President Theodore Roosevelt, resulted in the establishment of a French protectorate over Morocco, except for a small area placed under Spanish protection and an internationalized enclave at Tangiers.

French control of Algeria, Tunisia and Morocco was undisturbed by any major rebellions until after the conclusion of World War II.

The only country in the Maghreb whose destiny was directly affected by either of the great conflicts was Libya, part of which became an Italian protectorate in 1904, and was later extensively developed as a colony by Mussolini.

After the defeat of the Axis Powers, Italy was forced to surrender its recent conquest of Ethiopia and to place Libya under United Nations Trusteeship.

The Maghreb Revolt

The revolt of the North African Arabs against France, long-simmering but repressed by police-state measures, first broke out into the open in Morocco in 1950. The conditions which inspired the rebellion were common to all of French North Africa.

The population of French Morocco was roughly 9,000,000, of which 350,000 were French and other European settlers. This European minority managed, controlled and ruthlessly exploited the Moorish majority. During their forty years of occupation, the French made many physical investments and improvements, but their development schemes were designed exclusively for their own benefit. They built an economy based upon discrimination in which the Europeans owned the best land, most of the mines and practically all the industries. The Moors were the serfs, living in slums and performing menial labor. Wage scales were, with few exceptions, openly discriminatory. There were only about two dozen primary schools for the entire Moorish population. Child labor was viciously exploited. Education, like every other sort of privilege, was reserved for the French. In the words of Justice William O. Douglas, written after a visit to North Africa, "The French have fastened a milking machine on Morocco for their own benefit." *

In 1950, Sultan Sidi Mohammed V proposed some mild and long overdue reforms. He did not seek to expel

* *Look,* October 19, 1954.

the French; in fact, he proposed to guarantee them against expropriation. He demanded an educational program, a free press, freedom of assembly and freely elected representative government. He asserted the right of Moorish labor to form trade unions.

The French broke with the Sultan over these moderate demands, using force and terror to repress a strike and to maintain their police state rule. The *Istiqlal* nationalist party was outlawed and many of its leaders jailed. In 1953, Marshal Juin, appointed as Resident-General to suppress the growing revolt, arranged a coup d'etat with the help of Thami El Glaoui, the powerful Berber pasha of Marrakesh. The Sultan was deposed and sent into exile; his unpopular cousin, Moulay Mohammed ben Arafa, was installed in his place. From then on, relations between the Moors and the French went from bad to worse, leading eventually to the bloody disorders of August, 1955. The new Sultan agreed to "reforms" which were purely nominal and served merely to increase the spirit of revolt. New "popular assemblies" were, for example, created in which the French minority was given the right to elect half the members. The French continued to control the bureaucracy and the police, backed by ever greater military forces. Probably the only reason why the French colons refrained from demanding the establishment of complete French sovereignty was that this would have subjected their profits to French taxation.

From Morocco, the spirit of revolt spread to Algeria and Tunisia. The 8,500,000 Algerian Moslems are theoretically "French citizens," but of the 30 representatives Algeria sends to the National Assembly in Paris, 15 are elected by the French settlers. So also in the local Algerian

Assembly, half the delegates are elected by the colons. The law establishes "equality" but one Frenchman's vote is equal to that of eight Moslems. Like the *Istiqlal* in Morocco, the Algerian MTDL* and the Tunisian *Neo Destour* were outlawed. A French army of some 200,000 soldiers, equipped with tanks and artillery held down the three nationalist movements. French North Africa became another Indo-China in the making.

None of the postwar French governments made any serious effort to deal with this explosive situation until Pierre Mendès-France came into office in May, 1954. Many political leaders publicly condemned the deposition of the Sultan of Morocco. The majority of the French people were as unsympathetic toward their government's North African policy as they were toward its policy in Indo-China. Yet the power of the colons, of the business and financial interests allied to them, and of their political lobby was such that no French government could see its way clear to break with the past.

In 1954, with Tunisia momentarily the focus of rebellion, Mendès-France moved to grant the protectorate autonomy within the French Union. Even this moderate proposal infuriated the colons. One of the key figures in the parliamentary intrigue which brought about the fall of Mendès-France was a former premier, René Mayer, whose constituency lies in Algeria. Edgar Faure, succeeding Mendès-France, eventually managed with the help of Tunisia's remarkable leader, Habib Bourguiba, to put through Tunisian autonomy. By this time—April 1955— all of French North Africa was seething with revolt and demanding independence. When after months of bloody

* Movement for the Triumph of Democratic Liberties.

incidents in Morocco, Premier Faure finally moved to depose the unpopular Moulay ben Arafa and to establish a regency, it was already too late for anything less than the granting of complete independence. This was finally conceded to Morocco and Tunisia in 1956.

The long-smoldering Algerian revolt broke out into the open on November 1, 1954, with 30 assaults in various parts of Algeria, the setting of fires and the explosion of bombs. The failure of more than a century of French effort to build an extension of France on African soil was due to three major reasons: the resistance of Islam, not merely as a religion but as a way of life; the selfishness of the French settlers; and the tremendous increase of the native population.

The oppression of the Moslem majority of 8.5 million by the European minority of 1 million (700,000 of whom are French) created an ever-growing proletariat which formed the ideal breeding-ground for anti-French nationalist sentiment. It required only the Moroccan and Tunisian rebellions to touch off the explosion.

Prior to World War II, the French had dealt with occasional nationalist leaders, like Messali Hadj in 1926 or Ferhat Abbas some years later, by the simple expedient of exiling them or clapping them into jail. (Habib Bourguiba, the liberator of Tunisia, told the writer that he had spent over 20 years of his life in French prisons.) In 1947, the Socialist cabinet of Paul Ramadier made a feeble effort to effect reforms in Algeria which might appease the growing nationalist movement. These measures were rejected by even the most moderate nationalist leaders. Moreover, what little effect they might have had was offset by the authoritarian rule of Governor-General

Naegelen and his successor, Léonard, a former Paris Prefect of Police.

When the revolt broke out, in November, 1954, Premier Mendès-France announced his intention to defend Algeria and sent in French troops to suppress the revolt. This response was probably conditioned in part by Mèndes-France's desire to win support for his moderate policy in Tunisia by drawing a sharp distinction between granting autonomy to a protectorate and permitting a nationalist movement to make headway in a part of Metropolitan France. Whatever the motivation, the sending of the first troop reinforcements set off a vicious circle.

In the following year, Premier Faure called up reservists and raised the number of troops in Algeria to 180,000 —and still the rebellion grew. When the government of Guy Mollet came to office, in February, 1956, the situation was already out of hand. The new Resident Minister Robert Lacoste—a follower of Charles de Gaulle—came to Algiers without any program other than suppression by force. By July, 1956, he had withdrawn practically all of the French troops assigned to NATO and raised the total of French forces in Algeria to over 400,000. The revolt had now reached a point at which France felt compelled to sacrifice her own military security and her prestige in NATO to the pacification of Algeria.

The reforms which Lacoste offered were both much too little and much too late. By this time, any Moslem who might accept a government post or a share in redistributed land made himself a candidate for assassination.

So far as land ownership was concerned, the government actually redistributed some 80,000 hectares expropriated from two private companies, but this was a mere drop in the bucket. According to the most recent figures, 1.7 million out of 4.4 million hectares of cultivable soil still belonged to 44,000 European families, while 6.5 million Moslems—about half of them landowners and the rest tenant sharecroppers or laborers—were crowded together on the remaining land.*

Unlike Morocco, Algeria has few raw materials and, since power costs 40% more than in France, there has been little industrial development.

Meanwhile, some 360,000 Moslem children are born in Algeria each year.

The strain imposed upon France by her stubborn colonial policy is undermining not only her military power but her domestic economy. "Pacification" is costing the French Treasury about $1 billion a year.

Worst of all, the attempt to suppress the Algerian revolt is eating away the goodwill acquired by France in the two former protectorates which she has belatedly liberated. Not only has French policy in Algeria stood in the way of the development of a Western-oriented Arab federation in North Africa; it has also endangered the French hold upon the territories to the South. Unless the Algerian question is settled soon, France may lose Mauritania to an alienated Morocco and the newly discovered mineral wealth in the Sahara to an unfriendly Algeria.

What France does or fails to do in the Maghreb vitally affects the future of Western relations to the entire Arab world.

* Reto Caratch in the April, 1957, issue of the *Swiss Review of World Affairs*.

THE MORE RECENT

BACKGROUND OF

THE CRISIS

In considering the more recent history of the Middle East one is struck by the fact that the present violently anti-Western feelings of the Arab peoples are almost entirely the product of the last 39 years. It is true that some residue of ancient anti-Western feeling probably remains from the religious wars of the past, and from the fact that Islam is a different way of life. But, in 1918, when the Arab peoples of Asia Minor were liberated by the Allies from centuries of Turkish rule, these ancient memories and religious prejudices were all but expunged and the Western powers were regarded throughout the area as liberators. At this moment, Western prestige and influence stood at an all-time high.

The ensuing 39-year period, during which Western prestige has sunk to an all-time low in modern history,

falls into two parts. The first runs from the break-up of
the Ottoman Empire in 1918 to the end of World War II.
The second extends from the conclusion of World War II
down to the present.

During the first period, the United States had little or
nothing to do with the decline of Western influence;
during the second period it bears a major share of the
responsibility.

I

The Interwar Period
Origin of Arab Anti-Westernism

In return for their participation in the war against
Turkey, the Arab peoples were promised independence
by Britain. This pledge was given to the Sharif of Mecca,
later King Husain of the Hejaz, by Sir Henry McMahon
in 1915. The promise did not apply to the British protectorate of Aden, nor to the colony of Aden which had
been annexed to India in 1839. McMahon also made a
vague reservation as to French interests in Syria and the
Lebanon.

The British did not inform their allies of this agreement by which they obtained active Arab support for their
campaign against the Turks. On the contrary, a few
months later they secretly entered into the notorious
Sykes-Picot Agreement under which Britain, France and
Russia proposed to divide among themselves Asia Minor
and most of the Arab peninsula. The publication of this
agreement by the Bolsheviks in December 1917 aroused
the first serious suspicion and distrust among the Arab
peoples.

At the Versailles Peace Conference, the Sykes-Picot

agreement was officially scrapped. Russia had dropped out of the picture. France gave up her claim to the Iraqi province of Mosul in exchange for a share of its oil production but was promised a League of Nations mandate over Syria, including the Lebanon. Britain was awarded the mandates over Palestine (including Jordan) and Iraq. Meanwhile, Sharif Husain, who had proclaimed himself "King of the Arab Nation" was ousted from his throne by King Ibn Sa'ud and the Hejaz was annexed by Sa'udi Arabia which had already swallowed up two other neighbors, 'Asir and Shammar.

The fate of Syria and Iraq was not settled until after a long and bitter struggle. The British at first installed Faisal, Husain's eldest son, as King of Syria, but in 1920, at the San Remo Conference, Clemenceau succeeded in having his way and a French mandate was established over Arab protest. Faisal resigned and, a year later, after the Iraq revolt had been suppressed, was installed by the British as King of Iraq.

The kingdom of Jordan was arbitrarily created by Britain for Faisal's brother, Abdullah. Both Hashemite Kingdoms as well as the smaller sheikdoms of the Arabian peninsula, though nominally independent, were actually under British influence and protection. Thus the only Arab states to obtain immediate independence were the two most backward countries, Sa'udi Arabia and Yemen.*

This is where a large part of the trouble began. The League of Nations mandates were conceived by President Wilson as trusteeships under which the mandated terri-

* For a full account of the Arab betrayal, see George Antonius, *The Arab Awakening,* Chapters 13 and 14; Hamish Hamilton, London, 1938.

tories were to be prepared for independence. However, over Wilson's unavailing protest—weakened by American rejection of the League—these mandates were distributed either in accordance with the secret treaties entered into by the Allies prior to American entry into the War, or to those of the victors who had "liberated" the respective territories. Thus, in many cases, the mandates came to be regarded as spoils of war, rather than as trusteeships for the benefit of the peoples concerned.

In this respect, the French were the worst offenders. Their policy in the Middle East, as elsewhere, was directed toward permanent dominance or possession, rather than toward fostering the emergence into independence of mandated territories or protectorates. Syria and Lebanon were emancipated from French rule only when the Vichy forces were driven out by the British and Free French during the course of World War II.

On the other hand, British policy in the Middle East aimed not at permanent possession but at the creation of semi-independent states and principalities whose feudal rulers would be linked by self-interest to the British Empire. Britain's early troubles in the Middle East arose less from possessive colonialism than from conflicting promises, especially over the future of Palestine. In the McMahon correspondence with the Sharif of Mecca (later King Husain of the Hejaz) Britain had implied that Palestine should become a part of free and independent Arabia, but she had also, in the Balfour Declaration of 1917, promised the Jews a national home in Zion. These promises were not originally irreconcilable, since "a national home in Palestine" did not necessarily imply that Palestine or any part of it should become a politically independent Jewish state. In 1919, Husain's son, Faisal, declared to Dr. Chaim Weizmann:

> "The Arabs, especially the educated among us, look with the deepest sympathy on the Zionist movement. Interested parties have been enabled to make capital out of what they call our differences . . . I wish to give you my firm conviction that these differences are not questions of principle but matters of detail and are easily dispelled by goodwill."

Jews and Arabs—Origin of Political Zionism

Neither the Jews nor the Arabs are primarily responsible for the deterioration of their ancient amicable relationship. The chief burden of responsibility rests upon those nations which have caused bitter hostility to arise between two formerly friendly peoples. Those nations are Great Britain, France, Tsarist Russia, Nazi Germany and the United States.

This may seem like a strange statement, since most people nowadays attribute the Arab-Israeli conflict either to belligerent and irrational Arab nationalism or to intransigent Zionism, or to a combination of the two.

The fact is that political Zionism, like pan-Arab nationalism, was created by the past behavior of governments and peoples which professed the Christian faith but failed to practice the principles of Christianity.

If we examine the history of the past, we find very little evidence of hostility between Jews and Arabs. On the other hand, we find a long history of Christian hostility toward both the "Muslim infidels" and the dispersed and despised people of the Jewish faith. From the beginning of the Diaspora, in the first century of the Christian era, the Jews scattered throughout the Christian countries of Europe were treated as an undesirable, alien minority, to be segregated, denied most of the rights of citizenship and often physically persecuted. By contrast, during the seven centuries of Arab rule in Asia Minor, North Africa and the Iberian peninsula, the Jewish people living in this area enjoyed a high degree of respect and equality. When the Arabs were, in turn, conquered by the Turks, the Jews continued to be treated much as they had been under Arab rule. For about four centuries, Arabs and Jews lived side by side under a Turkish regime which, though at times and in some respects oppressive, made little distinction between the two subject peoples.

(Compare this with the fate of the Spanish and Portuguese Jews under the Inquisition, after Christian conquerors had driven the Moors from Spain.)

Hostility between Arabs and Jews began only when Jews living under intolerable conditions in parts of the Western Christian world conceived the idea of establishing a refuge in Arab Palestine. This movement, called Zionism, originated from an ancient religiously inspired impulse but, in its political form, was essentially the direct product of Christian persecution.

Political Zionism made relatively little progress during the late 19th and early 20 centuries because of the increasingly liberal treatment of Jews in most of Western Europe —in contrast to the chronic endemic anti-Semitism in Eastern Europe—and because of the safety-valve provided by unrestricted emigration to the United States. This safety-valve was practically shut off, particularly for the East European Jews who most needed it, by the American restriction of immigration and the imposition of the quota system in 1924. Shortly thereafter, the revival of virulent anti-Semitism in Germany and the Nazi program of extermination converted Zionism from a latent semi-religious movement into an irresistible political force.

Thus, the origin of political Zionism lies not in any inherent Jewish nationalism but in the un-Christian behavior of such Christian nations as Tsarist Russia, Poland and Rumania, with Nazi Germany capping the climax. These nations were the chief modern inheritors of the tradition of anti-Semitism which had permeated the Holy Roman Empire and most of the early Christian world.

Insofar as the Balfour Declaration was not a political warfare move, designed to win the allegiance of Jews everywhere and especially in the enemy countries, it was an act of penitence—an attempt on the part of one of the Christian nations to make up, at Arab expense, for what the Western Christian world had done to the Jews. Unfortunately, the Balfour Declaration started a chain reaction which led to the evolution of extremist political Zionism as well as to extremist Arab opposition to any kind of Jewish immigration.

Had it not been for the development of these extremist positions and, later, for the Nazi persecutions and the eviction or flight from Europe of large numbers of Jews, it is quite possible that a Jewish homeland in Palestine might have been established without serious friction with the Arab population. The solution might well have been found in the creation of a binational Palestinian state, as advocated by the late Judah L. Magnes, then president of Hebrew University.

The British handling of the mandate, however, discouraged any such development. Proceeding, much as in India, on the principle of "divide and rule," the British administration deliberately kept the two elements of the population apart, playing off the one against the other. Thus the tensions were exacerbated. From the Arab point of view, the British permitted Jewish immigration to become a menace to Arab sovereignty over Palestine and to Arab landholding. From the Jewish point of view, British restriction of immigration appeared as a heartless appeasement of the Arabs for the sake of an Empire policy primarily concerned with safeguarding British communications with India.

Even prior to World War II, the pro-Arab tendency on the part of the mandatory power was magnified by the discovery of oil in the Persian Gulf area, by the growing commercial and strategic importance of oil and by Britain's increasing dependence upon Arab goodwill for concessions.

II
The Post World War II Period

With the outbreak of World War II, the Middle East became a vitally important area, partly because of the Axis drive against Egypt and partly because Iran formed a vital link between the Western Allies and the Soviet Union.

Prior to that conflict, American interests in the Arab countries had been confined to the establishment of missions and educational institutions and, more recently, to the efforts of American oil companies to obtain a share of Middle Eastern oil production. World War II for the first time brought the United States into the Middle East as a major power.

Because of its preponderant economic strength, the United States gradually became the dominant factor in the war-time Middle East Supply Center, but left the political implications of this important operation largely in the hands of the British. This was where American power first became committed to the support of British imperialism.

During the War, Nazi propaganda skilfully exploited the resentments created by British politico-economic controls as well as the anti-French sentiments created by French colonialism and by the defeat of France at the hands of Germany. In addition, Dr. Goebbels, aided by the Mufti of Jerusalem, lost no opportunity to fan both anti-Semitism and Islamic anti-Westernism on religious grounds.

The greatest blow to Western prestige resulted, however, from the collapse of European power in the Far East before the onslaught of an Asian conqueror—Japan.

At the end of World War II, the Western position in the Arab Center was somewhat precarious but still far from hopeless. The Western powers no longer enjoyed the prestige of liberators. This time, their victory had brought the Arab peoples few recognized benefits. On the contrary, the arrangements made by the great Western oil combines with the feudal and oppressive Arab potentates had already begun to widen the gap between the increasingly wealthy few and the impoverished masses. Nevertheless, the flames of an overt, nationalist, anti-European revolution, already burning in Asia at the war's end, had not yet spread to the Middle East. And, so far as the United States was concerned, it still remained to be seen whether this great and powerful nation was to be considered a friend of liberating revolutionary change or *status quo* power.

From the Western point of view, the postwar era in the Middle East began rather auspiciously with sucessful holding actions against Soviet incursion in Iran and Turkey, the two non-Arab flanking countries of the Arab Center. Both countries had, as we have noted, long been objects of rivalry between Russia and the Western Powers. For two centuries, Russia had been knocking at the door of Persia, seeking access through the Persian Gulf to the Indian Ocean, and at the door of Turkey, seeking control of the Turkish Straits and egress to the Mediterranean. For two centuries, Russia had been blocked by Britain or by the concert of the European powers.

With British power waning after World War II, the Soviet Union renewed the Tsarist drive toward the South.

Iran had, during the war, served as a vital corridor through which much-needed American supplies were able to reach the Russian armies fighting in the South. At the war's end, Northern Iran was, once again, occupied by Soviet forces while British troops occupied the southern portion. Both powers agreed to withdraw by a certain date in 1946, but Russia failed to live up to her agreement. It was no small triumph for the newly founded United Nations to compel Russian withdrawal.

On the other Arab flank, Turkey was menaced by Soviet demands for joint Russo-Turkish control of the

Dardanelles and for a cession of border territory. Here American intervention in 1947 enabled Turkey to stand its ground.

Both of these actions redounded to Western prestige throughout the Middle East, but Western and especially American influence were seriously damaged by developments in the Far East and in Palestine.

The unsuccessful American intervention in the Chinese civil war, continued American support of the Nationalist regime after its flight to Formosa, American support of European colonialism in Asia—especially of French colonialism in Indo-China—caused the United States to appear as the most powerful defender of the *status quo.* British action in freeing India, Pakistan, Burma and Ceylon came too late to counteract the impression that the Western powers as a whole stood against the Asian revolution; and the more the Asian revolution succeeded, the greater became its influence upon the peoples of the Middle East.

Confused American Policy

No less disastrous to Western prestige were the events in Palestine. For these, the United States was largely though not solely responsible. It was under American pressure that Britain finally gave up its mandate and that the United Nations partitioned Palestine and created the state of Israel. This, in itself, need not have permanently alienated the entire Arab world. The fatal damage was done by the failure of the United Nations to suppress the Arab attack upon Israel and to enforce a just peace, including its own decisions as to Israel's boundaries. This failure of the United Nations to go through with its own solution of the problem and to assert its authority was chiefly due to the vacillation and indecisiveness of the American government. The result was a damaging blow to the prestige of the new world organization and the creation of a situation in which both the Israelis and the Arabs had and still have just grievances.

At the time of the Palestine partition, oil had become a major factor in British Middle East policy. The greater the discoveries of petroleum products, the stronger became British determination to retain control of the Arab peninsula; and, the stronger this determination, the more British policy centered upon wooing the friendship of the Arab nations.

American oil companies had, of course, also entered the picture by this time, but the importance of Middle East oil to European and, hence, to American security had not yet been fully recognized. Oil company pressure upon the American government was not yet as effective as Zionist pressure.

The trouble with Mr. Truman's decision to sponsor the creation of Israel was not that he made it, but that he made it without apparently realizing that he thereby involved American Middle East policy in a serious inner contradiction. President Truman apparently was not fully aware that backing Israel's creation involved a direct conflict with his own conception of national defense through the military containment of the Soviet orbit, as well as a direct conflict with the American interest in Arab-owned oil resources. He took his action impulsively and not as the result of a deliberate decision to subordinate one set of interests to another. The basic conflicts within American Middle East policy did not, in fact, become apparent until our government seriously under-took to build a Middle East alliance. Had the choice been made deliberately, the futility of attempting to win the Arabs as military allies against Russia might have been realized before it was too late. This would have prevented much of the subsequent trouble.

As it was, the Truman administration became increas-ingly entangled in contradictory efforts. Having failed to enforce the original partition, it guaranteed the armistice borders which were, in many respects, wholly illogical. Having underwritten the armistice, it failed to enforce the United Nations resolution condemning Egypt's infrac-tion of the armistice by belligerent blockade. And, having thrown in its lot with Zionism in aiding the creation of Israel, the American government proceeded to seek ways and means of arming the Arabs as allies against Russia, not realizing that arms in Arab hands were more likely to be used against Israel than in defense against the Soviet Union.

When the Eisenhower Administration took office, it quickly converted a confused and precarious position into outright disaster. Far more preoccupied than his predeces-sor with military pacts and alliances, Secretary of State Dulles proceeded to act almost as if the United States had no commitment to preserve Israel's existence. Setting out to woo the Arabs, he endeavored to make it plain that the previous administration's pro-Israeli policy was a thing of the past.

The rapidly growing investment of American oil com-panies in the Middle East was no doubt partly responsible for this change, but in even larger measure, the pro-Arab orientation of American policy grew out of American preoccupation with completing, through a Middle Eastern military alliance, the band of physical encirclement by means of which it has sought to contain Sino-Soviet expansion.

One might have expected that these factors would have brought about the formation of a common Anglo-American policy. Such, however, was not the case.

For one thing, while both Britain and the United States had an important stake in Middle Eastern oil, their oil interests were also in competitive conflict. Thus, although the American government was helpful in settling the Anglo-Persian dispute, private American oil interests benefited considerably from the settlement. In Iraq and elsewhere, American and British oil companies were jealous competitors, even though they worked together in all sorts of ways to control production, marketing and prices. The oil interests of the two countries led them not only jointly to woo the Arabs at the expense of Israel but to vie with each other for Arab friendship.

A second divisive factor in Anglo-American Middle East policy arose from divergent attitudes toward the conflict between the European colonial powers and the rising nationalism of hitherto dependent peoples. This divergence of interest was brought to the fore by two events in 1951–1952: the Egyptian revolution and the Iranian rebellion against British control of Persian oil. Although traditionally opposed to colonialism, the United States, in its obsessive preoccupation with the cold war against communism, wavered between supporting the colonial policies of its military allies and sympathizing with the aspirations of the emerging peoples. Thus it gave enough support to Egypt to alienate the French and

British, enough backing to Britain and France to antagonize the Egyptians, enough help to Israel to antagonize the Arabs and enough arms to the Arabs to antagonize the Israelis.

In the Middle East as in Asia, the natural role for the United States would have been to act as the constructive moderator between the stubborn retentiveness of the colonial powers and the hyperfervid haste of the peoples seeking national independence. The American government failed to play this part chiefly because of its single-minded concern with building a military retaining wall against communism, often in almost total disregard of local sentiments, social conditions and political implications.

The outstanding example of this fatal obsession was Secretary of State Dulles' ill-advised attempt to construct a Middle East alliance which would link NATO in the West with SEATO in the Far East. After having urged the British to evacuate Suez and having personally presented General Naguib with the symbolic gift of a pistol, Mr. Dulles proceeded to sponsor the one idea predictably certain to make Egypt hostile to the West in spite of British withdrawal. This was the notion to rearm Iraq, Egypt's chief rival for Arab leadership and to link it with Britain, Turkey, Iran and Pakistan in the so-called Northern Tier Alliance. The product of this piece of cold-war strategy, the Baghdad Pact, actually created weakness rather than strength. The pact split the Arab world without erecting even the shadow of a military barrier to Soviet expansion. Worse yet, the rearming of Iraq caused Egypt to seek and obtain arms from the Soviet Union, thus opening the door to Soviet political penetration of the whole Middle East area. Soviet rearmament of Egypt, in turn, upset the Arab-Israeli balance of military power and brought Israel and Egypt to the brink of war.

The Baghdad fiasco shows how utterly foolish it is to arm nations against a danger the existence of which they do not recognize, especially when such nations have unresolved border disputes with their neighbors. The Pakistanis were not interested in obtaining American military assistance because they were afraid of a Russian invasion but because they wanted to strengthen their position as against India and Afghanistan. Rearming Pakistan has added little if any strength to the anti-communist *cordon sanitaire;* but it has dangerously upset the balance of power between Pakistan and its neighbors, alienating Indian sentiment and actually driving Afghanistan into the arms of the Soviet Union. Similarly, the Iraqis—unlike the Turks—did not want arms to defend themselves against Russia; they wanted arms with which to establish their hegemony in the Arab League and eventually to drive Israel into the sea.*

Faced with the collapse of his policy, Secretary Dulles at first made frantic efforts to forestall further Soviet penetration of Egypt by hastening American aid toward building the Aswan High Dam. In this, he was hampered by a reluctant Congress. When it became apparent that the Kremlin was in no hurry to outbid the United States

* Demaree Bess, in an article appearing in the *Saturday Evening Post* of April 20, 1957, presented a somewhat different version, according to which Dulles sponsored the Northern Tier Alliance *without* Iraq. According to Bess, the inclusion of Iraq was due to British insistence, as was Britain's own participation in the alliance.

for this costly and in some respects dubious project, Mr. Dulles reversed his course, abruptly withdrawing the offer of American aid and justifying this about-face by a statement which would have offended even a government far less sensitive than that of President Gamal Abdel Nasser. According to the authorized biography of Mr. Dulles by Jack Beal, of Time-Life publications, this action by the Secretary of State was a deliberate "gambit" designed to force a showdown in the cold war. Whether or not this interpretation is correct, it was hardly surprising that the Dulles action should provide the hot-headed Egyptian dictator with an excuse to seize and nationalize the Suez Canal.

If Mr. Dulles wanted a showdown, he certainly got it. The strange thing, however, was that the American government was totally unprepared to meet the crisis which it thus precipitated. According to Cyrus Sulzberger's column of April 7, 1957, in the *New York Times,* "the State Department's Policy Planning Staff didn't even have a position paper covering the eventuality."

When Britain and France reacted to the Egyptian seizure of the canal by threatening military action, Mr. Dulles was apparently shocked and surprised. During the succeeding weeks, in which he tried to restrain hasty action, Mr. Dulles was forced to improvise, since no policy had been prepared to meet this all too predictable set of circumstances. In doing so, the Secretary of State pursued a wavering, ambiguous and somewhat tricky course, seeking to manipulate and maneuver Britain and France toward an undefined peaceful solution, rather than to persuade them to adopt a clear plan of action. Thus he frustrated and angered London and Paris while, at the same time, leaving President Nasser in possession of a far-reaching diplomatic victory.

There was at least one available alternative which this writer suggested in a letter to the *New York Times,* dated September 12, 1956. The suggestion put forward was for the United States to break the deadlock by offering to place the Panama Canal under the same United Nations or other international control as that which the Western powers desired to see established at Suez. This idea was by no means original. At the Potsdam Conference of August, 1945, the United States had proposed the internationalization of all the important international waterways, including both Panama and Suez. Had our government revived this idea in September, 1956, the tragic developments of late October might never have taken place.

The Crisis Erupts into War

While the United Nations Security Council was debating ways and means to settle the Suez affair, the world's attention was suddenly diverted to the revolt of Poland and Hungary against Soviet domination. A new dawn seemed to be breaking over Europe. Soviet leadership was now confronted with a fateful dilemma; if it failed to suppress the revolt of its satellites, it faced losing control over Eastern Europe; if it used force to suppress the revolt, it would lose face throughout the world and, especially, in the eyes of the uncommitted peoples whose confidence it had been so successfully wooing. For the first time in the postwar period, the Kremlin appeared to be in serious trouble . . .

And then came the incredible events of October 29-31. Israel invaded Egypt. Britain and France seized the opportunity—if, indeed, they had not created it—of announcing their intention to occupy the Suez Canal Zone in order "to separate the belligerents." The United States found itself strangely aligned with the Soviet Union in denouncing the acts of its closest allies. At the very moment when the Soviet monolith was crumbling, the Western alliance fell apart. Three of the Western powers had undertaken armed action no less contrary to their obligations under the United Nations Charter than Russian armed intervention in Hungary.

Whether Israel's action was justified by necessity is a matter which must be left to the judgment of future historians. It is certain, however, that the invasion would never have been undertaken, if the United Nations, supported by the Western Powers, had enforced its 1951 resolution demanding that Egypt cease its acts of belligerency against Israel. Instead, the United Nations and the Western Powers had done nothing to end the Egyptian blockade of Israeli shipping through the Suez Canal and through the Straits of Tiran, nor had any effective action been taken to stop the inflammatory Fedayeen raids and Israeli reprisals.

Leaving aside the question of Israel's justification, as well as the as yet unclear question of whether there was French and possibly British collusion,* one fact is incontrovertible. Had Britain and France not committed the incredible blunder of launching their own attack upon Egypt, Israel alone would have inflicted a defeat from

---

* See *The Secrets of the Egyptian Expedition* by Merry and Serge Bromberger; Paris, 1957.

which Colonel Nasser would probably never have recovered. If Anglo-French-American relations had remained intact and if Britain and France had refrained from military action, Israel would have pulled the Anglo-French chestnuts out of the fire along with its own.

To say this is not to say that a complete defeat of Egypt by Israel would have brought peace to the Middle East. No one can say what would have happened, if Nasser had been overthrown. No one can say to what extent Russia might have intervened or what would have been the consequences of Soviet intervention. The time has passed when peace can be established anywhere in the world by means of a victorious war.

Confusion of Legalistic and Moralistic Judgments

Denunciation of the Egyptian invasion by a United Nations resolution sponsored by the United States and the Soviet Union, along with the solid Afro-Asian bloc, the Latin American bloc and—most painful of all—Canada, led to the abandonment of the enterprise by the British government. Sir Anthony Eden's decision to withdraw was doubtless influenced in great part by the storm of protest within Britain itself and by the Soviet threat to send "volunteers" to Egypt and to use nuclear weapons against the aggressors. France reluctantly agreed to a cease-fire and withdrawal.

Israel agreed to a cease-fire but sought unsuccessfully to obtain, as a condition of withdrawal, assurance of future freedom of navigation through Suez and the Tiran Strait as well as a guarantee that Egypt would not be permitted to reoccupy the Gaza strip. The United States took the position along with the Afro-Asian nations and the Soviet bloc, that Israel's withdrawal must be unconditional; otherwise Israel would profit from its illegal action. Eventually, under the threat of sanctions, the Israeli troops withdrew on the "assumption" but not on condition that these requirements would be met.

From the legalistic point of view, it was perfectly clear that Britain, France and Israel had, by invading Egypt, acted contrary to their obligations under the United Nations Charter. It was equally evident that Soviet armed intervention in Hungary was in contravention of the Charter. It was, therefore, legalistically correct to demand the withdrawal of the invading forces from Egypt, just as it was legalistically correct to demand Soviet withdrawal from Hungary. This action, however, ignored the moral distinctions. Even from the point of view of legality, it ignored not only the debatable question of whether Egypt had broken "the law" in seizing the Suez Canal but also the unequivocally clear violations of the Charter committed by Egypt in its belligerent actions against Israel— actions which had gone unpunished and only half-heartedly protested for a number of years.

From the point of view of morality, there surely was a distinction, almost wholly obscured by this legalistic approach, between the brutal suppression of a revolt against foreign tyranny and the exasperated but less brutal action taken by the invaders of Egypt. There was clearly a further moral distinction between the desperate action of Israel and the ill-advised invasion of Egypt by Britain and France. Did it serve our national interest or the interests of justice to place Israel, Britain, France and the Soviet Union in the same moral category? Did it enhance our prestige to take this legalistic stand, without regard to the circumstances surrounding each of the actions so self-righteously condemned?

Misconception of "International Law"

These questions gain importance from the fact that there is no international law in the true sense of the word. Nor can there be any laws binding upon national governments and peoples unless and until there is established some degree of supranational government. What we normally call international law is for the most part nothing more than a collection of treaties and agreements between fully sovereign nation-states. The Charter of the United Nations is not a law; it is a multilateral treaty. Short of war, it can be enforced only upon transgressors too weak to resist enforcement or upon those nation-states which are voluntarily law-abiding. In these circumstances, the existing rudimentary beginnings of international law lose their moral force when one transgressor is brought to book and another defies the "law's" authority.

The height of absurdity was reached when the Soviet government brazenly announced that it favored the imposition of sanctions on Israel to compel a withdrawal from Sharm el Sheikh and Gaza.

It was all very well for President Eisenhower to declare that "we cannot apply one standard to our friends and another to those who oppose us." This is morally correct; but, translated into policy, it amounts to enunciating an unenforceable doctrine, especially when coupled with the admission that a nation, such as Soviet Russia, must be exempted from enforcement because of its strength. If it is true, as President Eisenhower has also said, that there cannot be "one law for the weak and another for the strong," then, in simple justice, there can be no coercive enforcement against the weak so long as enforcement against the strong remains impracticable.

Impact of the Fiasco

The major results of the Egyptian fiasco were:

1. The restoration of the very conditions which had provoked the explosion, plus the blocking for about six months of the Suez Canal.

2. The strengthening of Nasser and of the Cairo-Moscow Axis.

3. The destruction of British influence in the Arab world as a whole and the jeopardizing of what remained of Britain's preferential position in Iraq and in the vital Persian Gulf area.

4. The creation of a serious cleavage within the British Commonwealth, the resignation of Sir Anthony Eden (partly for reasons of health), and the realization on the part of the British public that Britain was no longer a world power capable of independent action.

5. The arousing of resentment on both sides of the Atlantic with a consequent dangerous weakening of the central core of the Atlantic Alliance.

6. The weakening of the French hold upon Algeria and the diminution of the hope that there might emerge in North Africa a Western-oriented Arab federation as a practical counter-balance to the anti-Western Arab League in Asia Minor.

It should have been clear to the American government at the end of 1956 that these developments demanded a drastic re-examination of American policy not only with respect to the Middle East but with respect to the whole structure of American alliances.

Chronology of Postwar Developments in the Middle East

1945

March 22   Arab League formed with headquarters in Cairo with primary purpose of preventing creation of a Jewish state in Palestine. Formation of League encouraged by Britain.

1946

May 9   U.S. and Britain protest failure of Soviet troops to withdraw from northern Iran. United Nations obtains withdrawal.

August   Soviet demands for joint military rights in Turkish Straits rejected by Ankara.

1947

March 12   After Britain declares inability to continue support of Greece and Turkey, President Truman proposes U.S. military aid to both countries and enunciates the "Truman Doctrine."

November 30   Britain having renounced the mandate, the United Nations under American leadership votes to partition Palestine into Arab and Jewish states.

1948

May 14 — State of Israel proclaimed. Arab League armies begin invasion and are defeated in a war lasting eight months.

1949

February — United Nations negotiates Arab-Israeli armistice but Arab states continue border raids and economic boycott.

1950

May 25 — U.S., Britain and France issue Tri-partite Declaration guaranteeing armistice lines.

June 17 — Egypt, Syria, Jordan, Iraq and Sa'udi Arabia sign collective security agreement.

French refuse moderate reforms demanded by Sultan of Morocco.

July 19 — Egypt closes Suez Canal to Israeli-bound shipping.

1951

March 15 — Iran nationalizes Anglo-Iranian Oil Company.

September 1 — United Nations resolution demanding that Egypt cease blockade of Israeli shipping. Egypt refuses.

October 15 — Egypt declines invitation to enter Middle East Alliance.

1952

September 27   Military coup in Egypt results in King Farouk's resignation. General Naguib becomes premier.

1953

February 12   Britain and Egypt agree to end condominium over Sudan.

August 19   Mossadegh ousted as premier of Iran.

August 20   French expel Sultan Sidi Mohammed of Morocco and outlaw Istiqlal Party. U.N. Security Council declines to intervene.

October 15   Israel is censured by the United Nations for reprisal attack upon Jordan.

1954

February 25   Abdel Gamal Nasser replaces Naguib as head of Egyptian government. Naguib remains nominal head until November.

February 25   Army coup in Syria ousts President Shishekly.

March 29   Russia vetoes Security Council resolution demanding compliance with order to cease blockade of Israeli shipping.

April 2   Turkey and Pakistan sign defense pact.

May 19   U.S. signs mutual assistance pact with Pakistan, causing dismay in India.

July 27	Britain agrees to evacuate Suez Canal zone ahead of schedule provided by 1936 treaty with Egypt.
	Mendès-France takes up negotiations for Tunisian autonomy.
August 5	Eight international oil companies reach agreement for resumption of production with Iranian government.

1955

February 24	Turkish-Iraqi defense alliance marks final step toward Northern Tier Alliance, with Britain, Iran and Pakistan later joining in Baghdad Pact. Rearming Iraq inflames Egypt.
April	French grant Tunisia autonomy but Tunisia now demands full independence.
June	Shepilov in Cairo, secretly negotiating arms deal with Egypt. (Announced in September)
July 18-23	"Summit" Meeting at Geneva.
August 18	Leftist Shukri al-Kuwatly becomes Syria's president.
September 30	Algerian revolt having assumed serious proportions, question is brought before U.N. France walks out until Assembly drops matter in November.
November 5	France re-instates exiled Sultan of Morocco.
November 22	First formal meeting of Baghdad Pact Powers.

December 14	Libya and Jordan admitted to U.N.
December 17	U.S. and Britain promise Egypt assistance in financing Aswan High Dam.

1956

March 2	British General Glubb dismissed from Jordanian command.
	France grants independence to Morocco.
March 20	France grants independence to Tunisia.
March 9	British deport Cypriote leader, Makarios.
April 7	Spain ends Moroccan protectorate.
June 13	Last British troops leave Suez.
June 23	Nasser elected president of Egypt.
July 19	Dulles withdraws U.S. offer of aid for Aswan Dam.
July 26	Egypt nationalizes Suez Canal.
October 29	Israel invades Egypt.
October 31	Britain and France begin invasion. Canal is blocked.
November 2-6	U.N. demands cease-fire. Soviet threat of sending "volunteers." Cease-fire accepted. U.N. creates Emergency Force.
November 12	Sudan, Morocco and Tunisia join U.N.
December 22	Anglo-French withdrawal completed.

1957

January 5	President Eisenhower goes before

	Congress to propose "Eisenhower Doctrine."
January 19	Egypt, Sa'udi Arabia and Syria agree to replace British subsidy to Jordan.
January 22	Israel completes withdrawal from Egypt except for Gaza Strip and Sharm el Sheikh.
January 30	House approves "Eisenhower Doctrine." King Ibn Sa'ud visits Washington
February 2	U.N. demands complete Israeli withdrawal
February 8	U.S. obtains 5-year renewal of Dhahran air base in return for military aid to Sa'udi Arabia.
February 11	U.S. promises support for free navigation in Gulf of Aqaba
February 12	Russia proposes hands-off agreement in Middle East.
February 20	President Eisenhower says U.N. has no choice but to "exert pressure on Israel." Opposition in Congress to imposition of sanctions.
March 4-6	Israel orders complete withdrawal. U.N. Force enters Gaza. (Egypt appoints governor, March 11)
March 8	U.N. Force takes over Sharm el Sheikh.
March 9	President Eisenhower signs "Eisenhower Doctrine" as amended by Senate on March 5.

March 13	Britain ends alliance with Jordan and agrees to withdraw troops.
March 21	U.S. joins military committee of Baghdad Pact.
March 28	Makarios freed but not to return to Cyprus.
March 29	U.N. canal clearance partially completed.
March 30	Morocco and Tunisia sign treaty of alliance.
April 8	Canal cleared.
April 11	Sa'udi Arabia bars Israeli shipping from "territorial waters" in Gulf of Aqaba.
April 24	U.N. and U.S. efforts fail to obtain from Egypt satisfactory terms for use of canal. Egypt insists upon continuing to bar Israeli shipping.
April-May	Jordanian crisis, during which U.S. 6th Fleet is sent to eastern Mediterranean.
	Ibn Sa'ud draws closer to the two Hashemite Kings of Iraq and Jordan.

FIVE

THE DILEMMA OF

AMERICAN FOREIGN POLICY

During the dramatic events of October-November, 1956, the United States Congress was not in session. The American people were preoccupied with the last stages of an election campaign during which the administration played down the twin crises in Europe and the Middle East, while the opposition vainly attempted to make political capital out of a disaster which it had neither foreseen nor attempted to forestall. The United States did not wake up to the fact that it was in serious trouble until after the election; and, even then, the American people remained in a state of lethargic euphoria, induced in part by the let-down following a political campaign and in no small measure by the apparent unconcern of the greatly loved President whom they had so overwhelmingly re-elected.

The newly elected 85th Congress convened for the first

time on January 3, 1957. In spite of President Eisenhower's personal triumph, a Democratic majority had been elected to both Houses and it was, therefore, apparent that the Legislative Branch would play an unusually important part in the formulation of future foreign policy.

On the opening day of the session, the writer submitted to each Senator and Representative, as well as to certain officials of the Executive Branch, an analysis from which the following extracts are quoted.

(Memorandum to the 85th Congress) A New World and a New Dilemma

For the past ten years, the world has lived in the shadow of a power struggle between the United States and the Soviet Union.

The atomic stalemate has not ended this struggle. It has gradually transferred it from the military to the politico-economic arena. The two superpowers have been forced to realize that neither can overcome the other by military means. The result of this realization is what we call "competitive coexistence," which may be loosely defined as a competitive wooing of the minds of men throughout the world.

The weapons in this struggle are economic, political and psychological. The ultimate weapon is the establishment of a moral, intellectual and emotional position with which peoples in all countries can identify their beliefs, their hopes and their aspirations.

Within the past few months, each side has seriously undermined the psychological position which it has been constructing. The anti-colonial position which the Kremlin has sought to establish has been reduced to rubble by the brutal suppression of the Hungarian revolt. The moral position against aggression which the West has sought to establish went down the drain with the invasion of Egypt.

For the time being, the bipolar world has ceased to exist as suddenly as it came into being ten years ago. The Soviet monolith is crumbling. The anti-Soviet coalition is in the process of disintegration.

Each of the superpowers faces a wholly new and unfamiliar problem.

Recent events within the Soviet orbit may lead to evolutionary progress, or to regressive repression which might well be accompanied by adventures in external aggression. The Soviet regime may mellow under the impact of the revolution and survive in modified form, or else be overthrown in a convulsive death struggle likely to endanger the peace of the entire world. To a large extent the outcome depends upon what happens outside the Soviet orbit, and particularly upon the future development of American policy.

The crumbling of the Soviet monolith has its counterpart in the disintegration of the anti-Soviet coalition. This decay was dramatized but not caused by the Anglo-French invasion of Egypt. Its basic causes are to be found chiefly in a wrong-headed policy with respect to Germany, in the failure of the Western nations to agree upon a common policy with respect to China and the Middle East, and, above all, in the one-sided Western emphasis upon the military aspects of the power struggle.

Recent events, beginning with the Egyptian seizure of

the Suez Canal and culminating in the Anglo-French-Israeli invasion of Egypt, have brought into the open the weakness of the anti-Soviet coalition, just as the recent events in Poland and Hungary have exposed the weakness of the Soviet orbit.

The fact is that the United States now finds itself in what is perhaps the most serious foreign policy dilemma in its history. It faces the unsolved problems of the Middle East which brought about the events of October-November 1956. It also faces the unsolved problems of Eastern Europe. These Middle East and East European problems, in turn, constitute only one part of a much larger question which can no longer be brushed aside. That question reads:

Shall the United States accept as a fact that its interests and those of Britain and France are irreconcilable and, accordingly, seek a permanent alignment with the emerging peoples as the protector of their independence from both the old European colonialism and the new imperialism of the Soviet Union?

Or shall the United States assume that it still has an over-riding common interest with Britain and France and, accordingly, seek to rebuild the alliance, even at the expense of newly gained American prestige in the Afro-Asian world?

This is not necessarily an either/or question but, if a synthesis between these alternatives is to be found, the implications of each must be clearly understood. Both courses must also be weighed from the point of view of their probable effect upon American relations with the communist dictatorships.

I

The Case for Jettisoning the Alliance

Curiously enough, the most cogent argument for abandoning or subordinating the Anglo-French-American alliance has been put forward by one of Britain's foremost historians. Professor Geoffrey Barraclough, who recently succeeded Arnold Toynbee at the Royal Institute for International Affairs, has surprisingly advised the American people and their government that they have more to lose than to gain from maintaining the alliance. What the United States has to lose, he says, is "the possibility of a workable agreement with the peoples of Asia and Africa with the consequent risk of pushing them into the Soviet camp."

"America," writes Professor Barraclough,* stands at a crossroad when not to act is to be knocked down by the oncoming steamroller. "Yet," he continues, "the opportunities for decisive American action could not be better . . . It would take us too far to discuss the great strategic changes which have made NATO an obsolescent conception, but the political prospects opening out for American policy . . . are exciting enough.

"First of all, it should keep its eye firmly fixed on Asia; for it is there, and not in Europe, that the future lies . . . This fact alone requires a reshaping of American policy.

"Secondly, it is time for a re-thinking of America's attitude toward the 'uncommitted' nations, whose numbers are growing in fact if not in theory. Poland is a case in point . . . In spite of the setback in Hungary, we may

* In the December 1, 1956 issue of *The Nation.*

soon see in Central Europe what statesmen on both sides have refused to contemplate—a belt of 'neutral' states stretching from the Baltic to the Adriatic . . .*

"If the United States appears in Europe as the sponsor of Western Germany, it will never achieve a new relationship with Hungary or Czechoslovakia; if it appears in Asia as the ally of England, its relations with India, Burma and Malaya will always be troubled. Anything which appears like staving up the tottering British imperialism will breed anti-American resentment throughout the Near East, the Middle East and the Far East. Worse still, it can only prevent an evolution of American policy out of the past into the future . . . .

"The alignment with England and France was introduced to strengthen the United States in its relations with Russia. A continuation of it under present circumstances can only result in weakening all along the line. Far from obtaining security, America evidently runs the risk of being drawn, step by step, into an interlocked chain of incidents culminating in general war."

This advice from an eminent British student of world affairs will, no doubt, find a ready response among the neo-isolationists in this country who will grasp eagerly what Professor Barraclough says in derogation of the old European alliance but who will tend to ignore the equally important corollary concerning the need for an active, positive policy with respect to other parts of the world.

The entire article by Professor Barraclough deserves careful study, especially the following passage:

"Not the least of the long-range consequences of the

* Cf., the author's *Danger and Opportunity*, pp. 41-49, Current Affairs Press, 1956.

Anglo-French aggression against Egypt was the opportunity it created for a better understanding between Washington and Moscow. For one moment, before Soviet troops returned to Budapest, it even seemed that the hope Russia held out of an evacuation of the popular democracies had removed one of the principal obstacles to the establishment of more normal relations. That hope events in Hungary have dashed, at least for the present . . . but the Hungarian account is not closed . . .

"We do not need to minimize the issues which divide America and Russia to see . . . that neither belongs to the old world which has reared its head in a last dying convulsion at Suez. In social system and in human values, the Soviet Union and the United States are poles apart; but in international affairs, paradoxically enough, they have much in common. Above all else, they are attuned to a future in which Asia and the Moslem world will have a new part to play."

II
The Case for Rebuilding the Alliance

The following passage from a *New York Times* editorial of November 29, 1956, typifies the sober second thought which argues for a rebuilding of the alliance:

"With obvious concern over the rift in free world solidarity . . . Western statesmen are now taking steps to mend this rift, to iron out their differences and, above all, to save the alliances from serious damage. These alliances . . . are and must remain the principal bulwarks against the great menace of our days— the threat of continued communist aggression.

"This . . . applies especially to the North Atlantic Alliance. It is not only the mainstay of our other alliances; it is based on a common civilization with common ethical and moral values which have their roots in the Judeo-Hellenic-Roman heritage and have flowered into the democratic way of life. Any real impairment of this alliance can only encourage the Communists. Any collapse of it would open the floodgates to the Communist tide . . .

"British and French military action did not merely divide these countries and the United States; it divided the whole free world, the North Atlantic alliance, the British Commonwealth and British public opinion itself. Furthermore, it was not the first such division as witness the separate British policies toward Communist China and Taiwan.

"But if the alliances are to survive it is essential to put first things first, to agree on primary goals, and then, above all differences, to credit each ally with good faith. Surely, all the allies, including Britain, France and the United States, agree that the essential purpose must be to check further Communist aggression, and that the primary goal must be to do this without precipitating an atomic war. If differences arise as to the best way of achieving this purpose, then the remedy clearly lies in more intensive consultations. The machinery for this has heretofore been faulty, but the North Atlantic Council is now trying to improve it . . ."

The need for closer consultation and for the development of common policies has been emphasized by this observer on many occasions in the past. In an article appearing in the June 14, 1956, issue of *The Reporter,** a proposal was put forward for the creation of a new, non-military *Western Council* in which continual thrashing out of conflicting aims and interests would lead to the development of common policies, not only among the NATO powers but among all the nations of the so-called Atlantic Community. Had such a *Western Council* existed last October, Anglo-French action in Egypt without prior consultation would have been impossible.

In a more recent publication,** this proposal for a re-organization of the West was further elaborated, with special emphasis upon the need for drawing the Latin American countries into closer consultation and membership. Several chapters of this pamphlet were devoted to a discussion of how common policies might be arrived at with respect to Europe, Asia and the Middle East.

The chief needs emphasized in this discussion were:

1. The re-orientation of Western policy in Europe toward the creation of precisely such a neutral belt—including a neutralized, reunited Germany—as that envisaged by Professor Barraclough;

2. The re-orientation of Western policy in the Far East toward negotiation with the Chinese People's Republic and toward loosening the ties between Moscow and Peking;

3. The re-orientation of Western policy in the Middle East toward a withdrawal in circumstances which would insure the independence of the nations in that area and

* Inserted in the *Congressional Record* of June 12, 1956 by Congressman Henry Reuss of Wisconsin.
** op. cit. *Danger and Opportunity.*

prevent the Soviet Union from moving in on the heels of Western retirement; and

4. The development of a common, multilateral approach toward aiding the economic development of the emerging peoples of Asia and Africa, aimed at helping these peoples to achieve their aspirations without sacrifice of independence and self-respect.

Granted that a well-nigh fatal amount of time has been lost, the writer would venture the opinion that the task has not yet become impossible, even though recent events have made it vastly more difficult. One thing, however, is certain:

The necessary readjustment, which concerns primarily Britain, France and the United States, must not and cannot be viewed as a one-way street. If we expect Britain and France to agree to a retreat from the remnants of their imperial positions in the Middle East and North Africa, we shall have to retreat from our own isolated position with respect to the Far East. It is not Britain which has pursued "separate policies toward Communist China and Taiwan," as the *New York Times* would have it in the editorial just quoted. It is the United States which has pursued a separate policy approved by none of its NATO allies. Our right to Taiwan or Okinawa is far more questionable than Britain's right to Cyprus or French rights to the retention of Algeria.

III
The Crux of the Dilemma

This brings us to the crux of the dilemma confronting our government.

How can it make either choice without arousing so

much of the latent isolationist, revisionist, go-it-alone sentiment in this country as to frustrate the development and execution of *any* responsible foreign policy?

Any effort to rebuild the alliance is certain to end in failure, unless the alliance is rebuilt, not as it was, but in a broader, more closely-knit and essentially non-military form, providing for the hammering out of common policy with respect to all the non-Western parts of the world. This would mean that our European allies would have to make far-reaching and painful concessions in Africa and the Middle East which could reasonably be expected only if we were to make some equally painful concessions in the Far East. But, here, our government finds itself in head-on collision with the neo-isolationists to whom nothing—not even the vision of a "Fortress America"—is more sacrosanct than the American alliance with Chiang Kai-shek.

If, on the other hand, our government were to jettison the European alliance in order to free itself from associa-ation with colonialism and to develop an active champ-ionship of the emerging peoples, the sacrifice would be in vain unless we also jettisoned our present Far Eastern policy. We cannot hope to win the allegiance of the un-committed Afro-Asian peoples so long as we refuse to come to terms with the government which rules an Asian nation of 525,000,000 people—especially when that na-tion symbolizes to the dependent peoples the revolt from European domination.

Moreover, if we abandon the European alliance, our foreign policy as a whole will lose the support of the most active and influential "internationalist" segments of American public opinion. Without the support of these

elements, which sponsored the Marshall Plan and the
NATO alliance, it is almost inconceivable that our government could gain Congressional approval for the foreign aid programs which would be essential to making
the United States the chief magnet of political attraction
for the peoples of Asia, Africa and the Middle East.

In other words, without the European alliance as the
infra-structure of public support for *any* active participation in world affairs, isolationist-revisionist sentiment
would be predominant.

Thus, so long as the "Formosa-first minority" is permitted to intimidate both a Republican administration
and a Democratic Congress—so long as any discussion
of our China policy remains tabu—we shall be unable
either to abandon or to rebuild the Atlantic Alliance.
Much less shall we be able to develop a synthesis of what
is best in each of these alternatives.

In this observer's view, the only viable course is a synthesis of the apparently categorical alternatives.

Given the present state and the slow progress of our race
relations here at home, it is difficult to see how we can
expect, within a short time, to become the recognized
champion of the mostly non-white Afro-Asian peoples,
even if we completely dissociate ourselves from European
colonialism.

On the other hand, it is imperative for the United
States to identify itself with the emerging peoples rather
than with the preservation or restoration of an obsolete
world order. To paraphrase President Eisenhower's recent statement concerning aggression, we cannot have
one standard with respect to the imperialism of our
friends and another with respect to the imperialism of

our opponents. So long as we support the French in Algeria or the British in Cyprus, we shall be unable to oppose Soviet domination of weaker nations in Europe or in Asia.

Our first effort should be one of persuasion, not by sanctimonious preachment or unfair economic pressures, but by an undisguised effort to help our friends to accelerate a retreat which has, in any case, become inevitable.

Algeria is a case in point. Every reasonable Frenchman knows that France cannot hold Algeria by force, any more than France could hold Indo-China. Every reasonable Frenchman is aware of how well the opposite French policy of moderation and conciliation has worked in Tunisia. Our job is to help the reasonable Frenchmen in overcoming the stubborn resistance of the colons, the militarists and the diehard minority, while at the same time lending our open support to the moderate native leaders in North Africa.

Similarly, our job with respect to Britain is to act in friendly awareness of the fact that the British people themselves are divided over such questions as Cyprus or Suez, and to align ourselves tactfully but openly with those wiser elements which have, in the past, brought about the withdrawal from India, Burma, Ceylon and the African Gold Coast. In such an effort, we should have the almost unanimous support of both the white and colored peoples of the British Commonwealth.

In the past, we have been inhibited from playing such a constructive, mediating part by our myopic obsession with the military aspects of the communist menace. We have thought more of bases, strategic positions and strategic materials than of the political conditions in a rapidly changing world. Because of this, we have become a *status quo* power.

If we wish to dissociate ourselves from European colonialism, the first step is to free ourselves here at home from the misconceptions which have been fundamental to our own postwar policy.

Apart from these considerations, which make us as yet ineligible to assume fully the role of the protector of the emerging peoples, it is necessary to ask ourselves whether it would not be unnatural deliberately to turn our backs upon that part of the world from which most of our ancestors have come, from which we derive our language, our literature and our religions, and with which we share so much of a common heritage.

It is not necessary to reject Europe in order to identify ourselves with the majority of mankind. It is necessary only to reject and dissociate ourselves from that part of the European tradition which symbolizes anachronistic power politics and obsolete colonialism.

Finally, unless and until we reach a better and more reliable understanding with Russia, it seems self-evident that the United States will continue to have a vital interest in preserving the independence from Soviet domination of at least that part of Europe which lies west of the Iron Curtain.

The time has come to seek such an understanding with the Soviet Union. Just as it is our natural function to facilitate the inevitable retreat of our European friends from untenable colonial empire positions, so also we should use every opportunity to build a bridge over which the Soviet Union may withdraw from its ultimately untenable position in eastern Europe.

(At this point the Memorandum referred to the Soviet proposal of November 17, 1956 and the writer's letter to President Eisenhower of December 7, 1956, quoted in Chapter 2.)

Should it be possible to reach an agreement with the Soviet Union with respect to Europe, the path would have been broken along which the United States could eventually become a wholly free agent in dealing with the problems of Asia, Africa and the Middle East. Assured of West European security, the United States would be at liberty to act without fear of weakening allies upon whose security its own security depends.

This is the key to our present dilemma both at home and abroad. A gradual, mutual withdrawal from Europe would not offend the isolationist wing of the Republican party. Nor would it, in the circumstances proposed, alienate that body of American opinion which fervently supports the European alliance. At the same time, a mutual pulling back out of Europe would set the pattern for the whole Arab-Middle East area; namely a Western retirement on terms which would preclude a Soviet intrusion into the vacuum thereby created.

Lastly, the beginning of a mutual withdrawal from Europe could also be the beginning of a serious approach to universal, reliably enforced disarmament.

IV
The "Eisenhower Doctrine"

On January 5, 1957, President Eisenhower took the unusual step of making a personal appearance before both Houses of Congress to deliver a special message, preceding the customary "State of the Union" message which he delivered a few days later.

The special message concerned the Middle East. Its emphasis lay almost exclusively upon the danger of Soviet aggression in that area. Specifically, the President asked the Congress to authorize him to use United States troops, if necessary, to help any Middle Eastern nation requesting assistance in repelling aggression by any communist-controlled country. Secondly, the President requested blanket authority to spend up to $200,000,000 as he might see fit in giving economic assistance to countries in the Middle East.

The declaration of January 5, became known as the "Eisenhower Doctrine," since it appeared to be an extension to the Middle East of the global policy, known as the "Truman Doctrine" which the President's predecessor had enunciated in 1947, at the time of his intervention in Greece and Turkey.

The House approved the resolution as submitted after a debate lasting until January 30. The Senate, after a considerably more exhaustive discussion, approved a modified resolution on March 5, which the House accepted and the President signed. The Senate rejected the requested *authorization* to use American armed forces, which was held to be inherent in the President's powers under the Constitution, and approved instead a simple declaration of policy, stating that the United States was "prepared to use armed forces" against any communist-controlled aggressor.

President Eisenhower's State of the Union message, delivered to Congress on January 10, 1957, was an eloquent statement of what is commonly called the internationalist point of view. Probably no Republican President had ever so flatly repudiated his party's traditional isolationism. Yet the President's expression of sincere concern for the establishment of world peace and for the welfare of mankind gave no hint of an American foreign policy designed to meet the radically altered state of world affairs. There was, in fact, nothing in the President's address which indicated that Mr. Eisenhower was aware of any need for a drastic policy revision.

In the Senate, however, it was apparent that most of the Democratic members of the Foreign Relations Committee were far from satisfied as to the adequacy of American foreign policy. Yet this powerful group of dissidents did not wish to break with a party leadership which still clung, along with the Administration, to the old concepts.

SIX

STEPS TOWARD PEACE

IN THE MIDDLE EAST

By no stretch of the imagination could the "Eisenhower Doctrine" be considered a definition of Middle East policy. A declaration of "So far and no further," backed by the threat of nuclear power, might perhaps prevent Soviet miscalculation and consequent overt aggression such as occurred in Korea. But such a declaration could provide no defense whatever against the far greater danger of increasing political penetration. The Truman Doctrine had not prevented the bloodless rape of Czechoslovakia. The "Eisenhower Doctrine" seemed most unlikely to save Syria from a similar fate, especially since Syria had already refused to accept economic aid from the United States so long as the United States backed Israel's right to exist.

The problem raised by Soviet penetration in the Middle East was quite different from that which arose in 1947, when Britain was forced to drop the defense of Greece and Turkey on the doorstep of the United States.

The Arab states had not asked for protection. Few, if any of them would accept an American protectorate in the existing circumstances. Any attempt to take over the British position, as the United States did in Greece and Turkey, would not only alienate the Arabs and drive them closer to the Soviet Union; it would also lose the newly gained goodwill of most of the Afro-Asian peoples.

In dealing with the Soviet threat, it is necessary, above all else, to have a clear view of the respective American and Soviet interests in the Middle East.

The United States has a very substantial commercial interest to defend because of the huge investment of its nationals in the oil fields of the Middle East. Even more important, the United States is committed to the defense of Western Europe whose economic life depends upon assured access to the petroleum resources of the Arab countries. In addition, the United States is committed to the preservation of Israel, the creation of which it sponsored.

The Soviet Union's primary interest in the Middle East is to remove Western military power, especially American power, from positions which, in the event of war, would threaten Russia's "soft underbelly." (The present state of affairs is comparable to one which would exist in reverse if Russia had bomber bases in Cuba and Mexico.) Russia has no need for Middle East oil, but the Kremlin no doubt has an interest—so long as the cold war continues—in making Western access to Middle East oil as precarious as possible. In addition, Russia has for centuries sought to gain control of the Turkish Straits and to break out into the Mediterranean.

Until the arms deal with Egypt in 1955, Soviet influence in the Arab world was negligible. Since then, the Soviet Union has been able for the first time to establish itself as a major power factor in the area.

Unlike the situation in Europe, where the United States could right now negotiate with Russia from a position of strength, the American government would in the present circumstances, have to negotiate from a position of weakness in trying to reach a satisfactory agreement with respect to the Middle East. This weakness arises primarily from three factors:

1. The Russians have the advantage that Arab nationalism is more anti-Western than anti-communist. With Anglo-French influence and power rapidly disappearing from the Arab scene, Arab anti-Westernism is becoming more and more sharply focused upon Israel.

2. The Russians are not committed, as we are, to preserve the existence of Israel.

3. In wooing the Arabs and pretending to be interested solely in their welfare, the Russians have no such clearly visible self-interest as we have through our huge investment in and Europe's dependence upon Middle East oil.

These are the great handicaps to our diplomacy which must be overcome before we can effectively negotiate a hands-off agreement in the Middle East. An additional factor working against us is our association in the Arab mind with the colonial powers, kept alive by our ambiguous attitude toward the Arab independence movements in North Africa.

Yet, in spite of these handicaps, the fundamental basis for a negotiation exists, because Russia wants us out of the Middle East no less than we want her out of it.

We cannot prevent Russia from filling the so-called

vacuum by attempting to fill it ourselves. We can prevent further Russian penetration only by negotiating with Russia an agreement permitting the Middle Eastern peoples to develop their full independence. This we cannot do, so long as our diplomacy remains hogtied by the unsolved problems of Suez, by Arab-Israeli hostility and by a system of exploiting Middle Eastern resources which creates inequalities and conflicts of interest within the area.

Unless and until the existing handicaps to our diplomacy are removed, Soviet penetration of the area will in all probability continue and, short of war, the United States will be powerless to prevent it.

I

The International Waterways

The protracted negotiations, conducted partly through the United Nations and partly by direct talks between the American ambassador at Cairo and the Egyptian government, have failed, as might have been expected, to break the deadlock over the Suez Canal. It seems most unlikely that President Nasser, backed by the Soviet Union, will relinquish absolute control over the waterway, unless some new element is introduced into the picture. It is equally unlikely that the European canal users will reconcile themselves to a situation which leaves the Egyptian dictator in a position to shut off their oil supply, or that Israel will reconcile itself to continued discriminatory blockade.

The unhappy result of an American policy concerned solely with halting the Anglo-French-Israeli invasion and with bringing about the unconditional withdrawal of the invading forces has been the restoration of precisely those conditions which provoked the invasion.

The means by which this deadlock could be broken are in American hands. There is nothing to prevent the United States from resurrecting in modified form its 1945 proposal for the internationalization of the world's strategic waterways.

When President Truman put forward this suggestion at the Potsdam Conference, Stalin was interested only in the Turkish Straits and the Kiel Canal. Churchill, according to Truman's memoirs,* did not want to discuss Suez. He explained that "the British had an arrangement with which they were satisfied and under which they had operated for some 70 years without complaints." To this, Molotov prophetically replied: "You should ask Egypt."

If the American government were now to offer to place the Panama Canal Zone under United Nations control and the operation of the Canal in the hands of the United Nations, provided that Egypt would take similar action with regard to Suez and the narrow entrance to the Gulf of Aqaba, it would become very nearly impossible for President Nasser to refuse.

Should the Russians raise the question of the Turkish Straits and the Kiel Canal, the answer would be that Turkey would be asked to take similar action only when and if an overall security agreement were reached with respect to the whole Middle East area; and that Germany would be asked to take similar action with respect to the Kiel Canal only when and if the Rhine-Danube waterway were placed under United Nations control.

* *Truman Memoirs,* Vol. I, pages 385-386, Doubleday, 1956.

When this suggestion was first put forward by the writer in September 1956, some six weeks before the Middle East crisis erupted into war, two objections were raised:

It was argued that there was no analogy between the "lawfully established" position of the United States as to Panama and the "illegal seizure" of Suez by the Egyptian government. As a matter of historical fact, there is an analogy; the procedure by which President Theodore Roosevelt acquired the Canal Zone in 1903 was so flagrantly in violation of treaty rights and international law that the United States, some twenty years later, paid the Republic of Colombia an indemnity of $25,000,000. Theodore Roosevelt himself made no bones about saying in his autobiography: "I took Panama." The whole unsavory story is told by Samuel Flagg Bemis in his authoritative *Diplomatic History of the United States*.* That, however, is not the point. Even if the American position as to Panama were impeccable, this would be no reason not to relinquish it in the interest of accomplishing our present purposes in the Middle East.

A far more cogent objection—cogent, that is, if valid —was that turning over the Canal Zone to the United Nations would seriously weaken the security of the United States. The facts, however, do not support this contention. Not being a sea-level canal, the Panama waterway is exceedingly vulnerable to enemy attack by nuclear weapons. A single atomic bomb could wreck one of its six giant locks and put the canal out of commission for months if not years. Worse yet, a single bomb could breach the Gatun Dam, turning Gatun Lake into a mud-

* Third edition, pp. 509-519, Holt, 1951.

hole and thus rendering the canal non-existent for a very long time. It is precisely for this reason, and because the locks will not accommodate our new supercarriers and supertankers, that the question of making the Panama Canal into a sea-level waterway has been seriously considered by the Rivers and Harbors Committee of Congress and by our military authorities. This project would, however, take about ten years and cost an estimated 4 to 5 billion dollars. These being the facts, it might well be that the Panama Canal would actually be safer, if owned and operated by the United Nations. It would certainly be no less safe, since its air defense would, in any case, have to be conducted far out over the Carribbean or the Pacific.

Having dealt with these objections, let us now see what could be gained by making the proposal.*

If the Nasser government could be persuaded to place the Suez Canal and the Tiran Strait under United Nations control, and if, in addition, Egypt and Israel could be persuaded to cede or sell to the United Nations a zone running from the Gaza strip on the Mediterranean along the Israeli-Egyptian frontier to the Gulf of Aqaba, the following objectives would be attained:

1. The Canal users, including Israel, would be assured of the uninterrupted availability of the waterway. They would also be assured of an alternative site for an additional canal and for pipe-lines running through neutral, United Nations controlled territory from the Red Sea to the Mediterranean.

* This was the proposal put forward by the writer in an article appearing in *The Reporter* of February 7, 1957.

2. A neutral zone would be established between Israel and Egypt.

3. By free transit through the neutral zone, a land bridge would be established between Egypt and the Arab states of Asia Minor.

4. By similar free transit, Israel would have access to the port of Elath and unimpeded entrance to the Gulf of Aqaba at the head of which Elath is situated.

5. The United Nations would have a suitable base for the maintenance of a permanent Middle East police force.

A plan of this sort becomes practically feasible only if the United States makes the opening move of offering to place the Panama Canal Zone under United Nations jurisdiction and control.

This is the key to the whole problem of Suez and to much of the problem of bringing about an Arab-Israeli peace settlement.

But what if the United States were to make the offer and Nasser were to refuse?

Nasser could not refuse without incurring the condemnation of every eastern and western nation interested in assured passage through the Suez Canal. He could not refuse without losing the support of the Arab states interested in selling their oil. If, in spite of these considerations, the Egyptian President should reject the proposal, it seems unlikely that he would long survive in power.

There is another aspect to this problem of the waterways.

Egypt and Sa'udi Arabia have claimed that the Strait of Tiran is "territorial water" through which there is no international right of "innocent passage." In spite of the American government's implied backing of Israel's claim to unrestricted right of navigation in the Gulf of Aqaba, both Egypt and Sa'udi Arabia have declared it to be their purpose to keep Israeli shipping from entering or leaving the Gulf. (The question is further complicated by the fact that Egypt claims to be exercising "belligerent rights" —a claim wholly inconsistent with the pretense of returning to the 1949 armistice agreement.)

Although the proposal here put forward would, if adopted, clear up the question of Israel's right of transit through both Suez and the Straits of Tiran, the United States might well take the lead in clearing up the much beclouded question of "territorial waters."

It should be brought to the world's attention that, if Egypt and Sa'udi Arabia can claim the Strait of Tiran as territorial water, Britain and France could by the same reasoning, shut off all traffic at the equally narrow mouth of the Red Sea, one side of which is in French Somaliland and the other in the British colony of Aden, with the British-held island of Perim in between. Similarly, Denmark and Sweden would have the right to close the narrow entrance to the Baltic.

Clearly, a new international convention concerning the world's waterways is badly needed.

The foregoing proposals would, if adopted, constitute a major contribution by the United States not only toward an Arab-Israeli peace settlement but also toward eliminating the threat to Europe's freedom and security arising from Cairo's hold upon its jugular. It was the seriousness of this threat which caused Sir Anthony Eden vainly to seek the formulation of a firm Anglo-American policy when he visited Washington early in 1956 before the seizure of the Canal, and which finally led to his desperate decision to invade Egypt later in the year. The American government, while rightly opposing the use of force, was strangely unconcerned about this threat to Europe's economic life even after it had become clear that more was involved than blackmail by a "little Hitler" who might sooner or later be brought to heel by economic pressure. Yet, once the Moscow-Cairo arms deal had been consummated, the West was clearly on notice that a far more serious threat was in the making; and when Nasser seized the Suez Canal, it should have been evident that the hands which had grasped Europe's jugular were, in effect, the hands of Moscow.

Given the failure to coordinate Anglo-American policy so as to deal with the situation in time and to prevent the fatal blunder of October-November 1956, it now seems that there are three alternatives:

To reach an understanding with Moscow and, via Moscow, with Cairo;

To devise means by which Europe may be made independent of Suez;

To inject a wholly new element into the negotiations which will break the deadlock.

These three alternatives are not mutually exclusive. Negotiation with Moscow concerning the entire Middle East problem is in any case necessary; the question is only one of timing and preparation. Alternative routes of supply are also in any case necessary, but they will take time to develop; new pipelines cannot be laid overnight, nor can a fleet of supertankers be suddenly created.

The one thing which could be done now is to inject a new element that would both pave the way for negotiation and facilitate the development of a safe alternative supply route.

The proposal advocated by the writer would accomplish both purposes. It could reasonably be expected to break the deadlock over Suez. It would provide a strip of United Nations controlled territory running from Gaza to the Gulf of Aqaba through which new pipelines could be laid, so that unlimited supplies of oil could be piped to Mediterranean ports. This would avoid dependence upon either Suez (which, even if rendered safe through United Nations control, would still be inadequate) or upon tankers too large for European terminals to handle. The much-needed additional supply route would be provided without antagonizing the Arabs by pumping oil through Israel from Elath to the Mediterranean, and without incurring the risks inherent in running additional pipelines through any of the Arab countries.

II
A Middle East Development Authority

A second step advocated by the writer some months ago, goes hand in hand with the proposal concerning the waterways and the establishment of a United Nations controlled Gaza-Aqaba strip. This second step relates to economic development.

In December, 1956, a group of independent British Middle East experts published a plan for the creation of

* In the London *Observer,* December 16, 1956.

a United Nations Middle East Development Authority.*
The basic assumption of this group was that there could
be no security from expropriation of foreign-owned oil
installations and no security against sabotage of pipelines
controlled by private oil companies, unless foreign development of oil resources acquired the firm backing of
Middle Eastern public opinion and recognized international law. The group put forward substantially the following proposal:

It suggested that by international agreement a United
Nations Regional Development Authority be authorized
to place a levy upon all oil shipments from Middle Eastern ports, and that, in addition, the Development Authority should take over and operate all Middle East pipelines,
charging an additional levy to cover operating costs and
existing charges for transit rights. The proceeds from
both levies would then be contributed toward an approved economic development program for the entire
area.

By this means, the authors of the plan contended that
the oil companies and the oil consumers would obtain
greatly increased and internationally guaranteed security
of operation. They would, admittedly, pay more for Middle Eastern oil than they had been paying, but "not as
much as it will certainly cost them if Middle East conditions continue as anarchic as they otherwise must
become."

If this were to be done, the authors of the plan contended that the Middle East countries would have a
sufficient stake in oil revenues to give them a strong
vested interest in uninterrupted production and marketing. Since their collective revenues would be channeled

through the United Nations, the Middle East countries would have reasonable assurance that these funds would be equitably shared and applied where they would most benefit the area, instead of being monopolized by those countries in whose territory the oil deposits happened to lie.

It goes without saying that the oil-rich countries and sheikdoms will at first be less enthusiastic for such a scheme than Syria, Lebanon, Jordan and Egypt. Nevertheless, Sa'udi Arabia, Iraq and the Persian Gulf sheikdoms will gain but little from their rich oil fields, if production and transportation are subject to continued threats or interruption.

In endorsing this plan,* the writer proposed an addendum; namely, that the United States should sponsor the creation of a United Nations Authority and offer to channel through it American contributions to the economic development of the Middle East area, provided that the Soviet Union would agree to do likewise. Were the Soviet Union to accept such a proposal, one of the major aims of a Middle East settlement would be achieved; to wit, the elimination of all political overtones from both American and Soviet economic assistance. Were the proposal to be made by the United States and rejected by the Soviet Union, the expansionist aims of the Kremlin

* *The Reporter,* February 7, 1957. Commenting upon this proposal, the editor of *The Reporter,* Dr. Max Ascoli, questioned whether the United Nations would be capable of exercising the functions allotted to it. The writer's reply published in the February 21st issue of *The Reporter,* was that, if the United Nations is inadequately equipped for this sort of function, the answer is to strengthen it. See Chapter 8.

would be unmasked and Russian influence throughout the area would be greatly diminished.

Russia Takes the Initiative

American sponsorship of this proposal, including the additional offer contingent upon Soviet acceptance, would constitute a further step in preparing the ground for a Middle Eastern settlement, but the precondition for such a settlement remained the opening of negotiations in Europe. Nothing had been undertaken by Washington to seize the opportunities presented by Russia's troubles in Europe and thus to forestall a Soviet initiative in the Middle East. This permitted the Kremlin once more to beat Washington to the punch.

On February 12, in a note addressed to the United States, Great Britain and France, the Kremlin took advantage of Western embarrassment, disunity and indecision by preempting the sponsorship of a mutual hands-off agreement in the Middle East.

The six points of the Soviet proposal were:

"1. The preservation of peace in the Near and Middle East by settling questions at issue exclusively by peaceful means.

"2. Noninterference in the internal affairs of the countries of the Near and Middle East. Respect for the sovereignty and independence of these countries.

"3. Refusal to undertake any attempts to draw these countries into military alignments with the participation of the great powers.

"4. The liquidation of foreign bases and the withdrawal of foreign troops from the territory of countries of the Near and Middle East.

"5. Joint refusal to supply arms to countries of the Near and Middle East.

"6. Assistance in the economic development of countries of the Near and Middle East, without putting forward any political, military or other conditions incompatible with the dignity and sovereignty of these countries."

Points 1, 2, 5 and 6—peaceful settlement of disputes, noninterference in internal affairs, an arms embargo and cooperation in providing economic aid without political strings attached—constituted a succinct statement of what should have been our own stated objectives, if our purpose was to assure the free and full development of the Middle East rather than to dominate the area ourselves. Point 6 is of particular interest in connection with the problem of economic development. A rejection of these four points would imply that we actually sought a dominant position.

On the other hand, points 3 and 4—abandonment of military alliances, withdrawal of foreign troops and relinquishment of bases on Middle Eastern soil—were clearly unacceptable because they called for one-sided concessions on the part of the West. The Soviet Union has no bases in the Middle Eastern countries, no known military alliances and no troops, other than perhaps a few technicians. Britain and the United States not only have bases and commitments under military alliances, but Britain also has a few troops in the Persian Gulf area where she still holds a Crown Colony and several protectorates.

The obvious *quid pro quo* for the neutralization of the Middle East, where the West holds certain positions which admittedly would threaten Soviet security in the event of war, would be the retirement of Russian coercive power from Eastern Europe. Had the United States assumed the initiative in proposing a concrete plan for the phased withdrawal of foreign troops from Europe, leading to the eventual neutralization of the Continent west of the Soviet frontier, the proper bargaining position would have been established.

On the day when the Soviet Middle East proposal was published, the writer stated the foregoing analysis in a letter published by the *Washington Post* and a number of leading newspapers across the country. The letter concluded with this warning:

"For us to reject the Soviet proposal out of hand— which is probably what the Kremlin wants us to do— would be the height of folly. What we should do is to accept in principle the proposed neutralization of the Middle East, stating, however, that we shall be willing to discuss the dissolution of military pacts, the withdrawal of troops and the relinquishment of bases only in the context of a corresponding Soviet withdrawal from Eastern Europe. Any other answer will leave us in a wholly invidious position in the eyes of the peoples of the Middle East."

Within twenty-four hours, our government brushed off the Russian proposal as an insincere propaganda move, designed primarily to make trouble for the Eisenhower Doctrine. This was the substance of the comment issued by the President's press secretary, James Hagerty, from vacation headquarters in Thomasville, Georgia, later amplified in a formal reply.

Whether sincere or insincere to the extent of being

merely a gambit in the battle for the minds of men, the Soviet proposal was unquestionably a shrewdly calculated move aimed at precisely that which it accomplished; namely, to put forward a proposal attractive to the peoples of the Middle East which the United States would reject.

The writer's article in *The Reporter* and his letter to the *Washington Post* did, however, arouse a considerable amount of interest in the Congress. Both were inserted in the *Congressional Record*. The letter was inserted twice— once by a Democratic Senator and once by a staunchly Republican member of the House.* The Administration remained impervious, but there was considerable evidence that the Congress, while willing to accept the "Eisenhower Doctrine" in modified form, was far from satisfied that this declaration would bring a Middle Eastern settlement any nearer. Nor were many members entirely happy with the expedient policy of catering to the bigoted and reactionary King of Sa'udi Arabia.

The question remained:

Would the growing realization that something more was needed result, in time, in the adoption of a more imaginative approach?

Peoples More Important than Governments

Obsessive preoccupation with physical defense against the assumed danger of invasion had, so far, led to a neglect of the historical, social, political and psychological factors affecting the area's potential for economic development. Concern for armaments and military alliances had

* *Reporter* article inserted by Senator Hubert H. Humphrey (D) of Minnesota, on February 12, 1957; Letter inserted February 20, 1957, by Senator Wayne Morse (D) of Oregon and on February 22, by Katherine St. George (R) of New York.

led to overemphasis upon relationships with governments rather than with peoples. Yet, peoples, not nations, are the key to the problems of the Middle East.

The Arab peoples are consumed with impatient and not wholly rational nationalism. Arnold Hottinger, a distinguished Swiss Arabist, has described this Arab nationalism as "romantic,"—as "a sort of spiritual disorder characterized by superficiality of knowledge, emotionalism, egocentricity and a lack of objective understanding and sympathy with things as they are." * Speaking of the lack of realism in this strongly emotional and high-pitched attitude, Hottinger says: "Instead of writing history, the romantic nationalist invents it."

This is doubtless an accurate description of the sort of nationalism inspired in ignorant street-mobs by such demagogues as Abdel Gamal Nasser. It is a negative nationalism, inspired not by affirmative purpose but by inflamed resentment distortedly focused against Israel rather than against a social order which has kept the Arab peoples in a state of backwardness. Moreover, this "nationalism" is not national in the strict sense of the word. Unlike the Persian, the Arab does not feel pride in and love for a nation-state. He feels a certain loyalty to his tribe and his village and—skipping over the nation-state—he feels a certain sense of cohesiveness toward the Islamic Arab world as a whole. His resentments submerge the real causes of his discontent; so much so, that he fails to see in progressive, democratic Israel a challenge to the very forces of reaction which hold him in subjection.

If Arab nationalism were truly nationalistic, the Arab peoples of Asia Minor would recognize that they are

* The Swiss Review of World Affairs, May, 1957.

already assured of national independence; that Britain and France are in retreat; and that the tiny state of Israel is no threat to their self-determination.

What is taking place in the Arab world is essentially a civil conflict—a conflict between the old order and the new—a revolt of the slowly awakening people against poverty and exploitation by feudal potentates or corrupt military juntas.

The lessons we should have learned in China are signposts for the Middle East.

We did not lose China to communism because of expansive Soviet imperialism. We lost China to communism because we did not understand the Chinese people, because the Chinese masses lay beyond the reach of our influence, and because we were thus unable to guide their revolution by demonstrating the availability of an alternative, other than communism, to oppressive and corrupt Kuomintang misrule. Because we were afraid of communism, we lost what little influence we had by supporting a government which the Chinese people were determined to overthrow.

If we lose the Middle East to communism, it will be for much the same reasons, but with far less excuse.

While rearming the Arab nations only makes matters worse, it does not follow that economic aid will necessarily have a beneficent influence. Money given or loaned to governments which are not responsive to the needs of their peoples will serve only to perpetuate the existing injustices and inequalities. Hence, the more economic aid takes the form of assistance to regional development, bringing direct benefits to the peoples of several nations, the more effective it will be.

The nature of the area supports this contention. Because of the shortage of water, only a small part of a predominantly agricultural region is suitable for cultivation. Only 5% of Egypt's land is arable. In Jordan and Sa'udi Arabia perhaps 10%; in Iraq 20%; and in Syria and Turkey, about 30% of the land is cultivable. Farming, except in Egypt and Israel, is primitive, undiversified and non-intensive. The sickle and the wooden plow are still in widespread use.

The vast majority of the Arabs are peasants owning little or no land and forced each year to surrender about 60% of their crops to landowners and usurers. In Egypt's fertile Nile delta, some 20,000,000 miserable fellahin average less than a single acre, while over one-third of the arable land is owned by less than 1% of the landowners.

15% of the Arab peoples are nomads. Less than 25% live in towns or cities. Industry, except for foreign-owned oil operations, accounts for less than 15% of national income.

According to United Nations estimates, per capita income in 1949 ranged from $40 in Yemen to $140 in Lebanon. This compared with $389 in the highly industrialized state of Israel.

Except in Iraq, where the government's oil revenues have been applied to a liberal development program, and Sa'udi Arabia, where the Arabian-American Oil Company has made major improvements, the people in the oil-rich Arab countries are little better off than the rest.

There is very little intra-regional trade. The few exports, other than oil, depend upon undependable world markets.

The Arab boycott against Israel hurts the Arabs more than the Israelis.

The whole region suffers from lack of water, which could be supplied in relative abundance only by cooperative regional development of river systems, such as the long-planned Yarmuk-Jordan development scheme.

These few facts will serve to highlight the problems involved in promoting economic progress. They indicate the limitations of government-to-government assistance and argue powerfully for a regional approach—especially for an approach which would spread the benefits of oil production throughout the area.

The linkage which now exists between the oil companies and the feudal rulers of the oil-rich lands constitutes one of the major obstacles to be overcome. This linkage has, without doubt, exercised a powerful anti-democratic influence upon the Middle East policy of the United States. Yet, surely, it is to the long-range interest of the oil companies no less than it is to the interest of the United States to see to it that the peoples of the whole region, rather than a few ruling cliques, benefit so much and so directly from oil production that they will not wish to interfere with it in any way.

The specific proposals put forward in this chapter would not solve the Arab-Israeli problem, but they might well contribute to its solution. If adopted, they would eliminate altogether the question of Israel's use of the waterways, reduce the likelihood of belligerent action and, above all, tend to integrate Israel economically in the Middle Eastern family of nations. There can be no peace so long as Israel remains an embattled bridgehead of the West. There can be peace only when Israel, while preserving its cultural and spiritual links to the West, becomes an integral part of the Middle Eastern community. As such, and only as such, can Israel in time become a welcome outpost of progress, social justice and democracy.

SEVEN

THE ARAB-ISRAELI QUESTION

It has been pointed out in an earlier chapter that Arab-Israeli hostility is of comparatively recent origin and that it has been caused less by the Jews and Arabs than by the nations of the West. Among the nations chiefly responsible, two have disappeared from the scene. Tsarist Russia with its cruel progroms has vanished; its place has been taken by an unpredictable and no less ruthless communist dictatorship. Nazi Germany has been supplanted by a divided German nation, at least one part of which has been seeking to make amends for the crimes committed against the Jews by the Third Reich. France and Britain, the prime movers in creating Arab anti-Westernism, of which Arab anti-Israeli sentiment is a byproduct, are still present; so is the United States which, though a late-comer, has contributed its share to the present state of affairs.

There is relatively little that Britain can do in the present circumstances to undo the harm she has done in the past, except to retire as gracefully as possible from privileged positions which have become untenable. Britain has already retired from Jordan. Her relations with Iraq, Sa'udi Arabia and the sheikdoms along the Persian Gulf no doubt require overhauling, but these relations have only an indirect bearing upon an Arab-Israeli peace settlement. The same thing is true as to Cyprus.

The French, on the other hand, are in a position to make two distinct contributions. They can cease their incitement of Israeli belligerency; and they can make their own peace with the Arabs in North Africa.

France has ceased to be much of a factor in Asia Minor. But, so long as France refuses to apply the lessons of Morocco and Tunisia to Algeria, she will continue to feed fuel to the flames of anti-Western Arab nationalism. Because the French government has, rightly or wrongly, considered that Colonel Nasser was largely responsible for the Algerian revolt, it has encouraged and supported Israeli belligerency toward Egypt. This has been a policy as contradictory as that pursued by the United States. French alignment with Israel has increased Arab hostility toward France; and French armed intervention against Egypt alongside of Israel has, far from helping the Israelis, prevented them from achieving the victory and the overthrow of Nasser which the French desired.

The greatest contribution which France can now make to an Israeli-Arab peace is to settle its own differences with the Arabs in Algeria. Arab feeling against Israel is not nearly as strong in North Africa as it is in Egypt and Asia Minor. Tunisia has a Jewish cabinet minister. The North African Arabs could, if Algeria were liberated, exercise a moderating influence upon the Arabs of Asia Minor.

Certain positive steps to be taken by the United States

have already been suggested. In addition, the American government should take positive action toward bringing about direct negotiations between Israel and its Arab neighbors.

As a precondition for such negotiation, the United States should ask Israel once more to make an unequivocal renunciation of territorial aggrandizement. The Israeli government has, on various occasions in the past, stated that it has no further territorial ambitions, but some doubt has been cast upon the sincerity of these declarations by Israel's attempt, after the invasion of Egypt, to retain administrative control over the Gaza Strip. Moreover, the uncertain future of Jordan makes it desirable for Israel to make clear that it will lay no claim to Jordanian territory even if that artificially created state should be partitioned.

Having obtained this assurance from Israel, the United States should take the lead in bringing about a United Nations demand that the Arab states enter upon peace negotiations. It should insist that every nation which voted to create the state of Israel has an obligation to insist upon Arab recognition of its existence and Arab willingness to negotiate a peace settlement. In a showdown vote in the United Nations Assembly, it seems unlikely that the Soviet Union would openly back a continued Arab demand for Israel's extermination. It is chiefly because the United States has taken no firm action that Moscow has been able to exploit Arab intransigence.

The terms of the peace settlement are up to the Arabs and Israelis, but a United Nations mediation board would undoubtedly be helpful, particularly with respect to the settlement of boundaries and the difficult problem presented by the refugees.

Concerning boundaries, one would hope that both sides would agree to certain readjustments of the armistice frontiers and that the Arab states would make no attempt to force Israel back to the lines set by the original partition. Any such attempt should certainly be opposed by the United States and by the United Nations on the grounds of both justice and practicability. One might hope that the adjustment of the present frontiers resulting from the Arab war against Israel would include the internationalization of the Old City of Jerusalem with its Holy Places and such other rectifications as would prevent the frontier from cutting through farms and villages or from creating wholly illogical and provocative salients.

The refugee problem requires third-party mediation, if only to ascertain the true facts. No one knows exactly how many Palestinian Arabs fled from Israel or how much property they abandoned. The fact that 70% of the land awarded Israel under the partition was state-owned considerably reduces the number of refugees entitled to compensation. One would hope that Israel would approach the matter in a spirit of willingness to repatriate or compensate those refugees who were actually displaced from personally owned property. But the number of Arabs Israel can absorb is limited; and Israel's obligation to compensate should certainly be reduced by the value of the property in the Arab states abandoned since 1948 by some 300,000 Jewish refugees, especially those expelled from Egypt, Iraq and Yemen. One would hope that the Arab states, once they have accepted the necessity for reaching a peace settlement, would cooperate in eliminating the refugee camps and in resettling within their borders those Palestinian refugees who either could not be absorbed by Israel or did not wish to return. Iraq would actually benefit from an accretion to its sparse population.*

The cost to Israel of compensating those of the refugees found eligible for compensation would be considerable. Realizing that Israel's greatest need is for peace with justice, there could be no more effective way for Jews throughout the world to help Israel than by contributing to the demands of justice. Beyond that, and without waiting for a final settlement of the refugee problem, it would seem to the writer that the American Jewish community could help to promote a peace settlement by extending some of its generosity to Israel's Arab neighbors—not, of course, by giving aid or comfort to governments still openly hostile to Israel. The writer has in mind the possible training in Israel of Arab doctors, nurses and teachers and the providing of exchange scholarships in primary and secondary schools. He has in mind what might be done with funds contributed by the American Jewish community for the innocent Arab children and for the youth of Israel by way of teaching them mutual respect and cooperation, instead of prejudice and hate. About half of the 200,000 Arab refugees living in the Gaza strip are under fifteen years of age. The same is probably true of the 500,000 refugees in Jordan. If these children were not only lifted out of their present miserable existence but helped to understand its true causes, a whole generation would be re-oriented toward peaceful coexistence. There is no reason why such private Jewish help could not be provided even before final arrangements are consummated

* For a useful summary of the refugee problem, see International Review Service, New York; Volume III, Report 31, issued in February, 1957.

for the repatriation or resettlement of these wretched victims of circumstance.

An Arab-Israeli peace settlement does not involve a reconciliation between traditionally hostile peoples. It involves the restoration of a friendly relationship which existed for centuries before it was disrupted by essentially extraneous forces. Both Jews and Arabs have commited mistakes and excesses. Yet both peoples are more sinned against than sinning. A new generation will bring forth its own leaders and these, given help, need not be infected with the spirit of irrational animosity so prevalent today.

The writer is well aware that these suggestions are easier to make than to put into execution. Yet the problem is there to be faced and solved for, without its solution, the whole Middle Eastern area will remain a seething caldron of animosity made to order for communist exploitation.

EIGHT

THE UNITED STATES AND

THE UNITED NATIONS

Up to this point, we have outlined a policy of disengagement in Europe and the Middle East, implemented by certain concrete steps. Since the success of such a policy will depend to a considerable extent upon working through and exercising leadership in the United Nations, it is now necessary to consider the relationship of the United States to that body. This subject falls naturally under three headings: 1) the overall attitude of the United States toward the world organization; 2) the role of the United Nations in a practical approach to disarmament; and 3) the role of the United Nations in promoting world economic development.

I
American Ambivalence Toward World Organization

The relationship of the United States to supranational world organization reflects a long-standing inner conflict between isolationism and world-mindedness. No nation has done more than the United States to create world organization. No nation has been more reluctant to participate in it.

At the conclusion of World War I, it was an American President who took the initiative in founding the League of Nations only to be repudiated by his own people. Again, toward the conclusion of the second great world conflict, the initiative for the founding of the United Nations emanated from Washington. It was Secretary of State Cordell Hull who, in 1943, flew to Moscow to obtain Marshal Stalin's agreement to participate in a new world organization to preserve peace. The drafting of the United Nations Charter took place at Dumbarton Oaks under American leadership. Yet so strong was President Roosevelt's fear that the American people might once more repudiate a proposal put before the world by their own leadership that the Charter was shaped as much from the point of view of assuring approval by the United States Senate as from the point of view of creating a world organization actually capable of "saving future generations from the scourge of war."

The antithesis between American leadership toward creating a world organization and American reluctance to participate in it reflects an inner contradiction which dates back to the earliest days of the republic. Thomas Jefferson was the author of a Declaration of Independence which enunciated the principles of a philosophy applicable to "all men everywhere"; yet he asserted no less forcefully than George Washington or John Adams the belief that the United States should avoid foreign entanglements. Since the birth of the nation, United States foreign policy has reflected the opposite extremes of idealistic universalism and pragmatic self-sufficiency.

Franklin D. Roosevelt was a less idealistic universalist than Woodrow Wilson. His world-mindedness was tempered by the cautious appraisal of the limits of the attainable. Where Wilson over-estimated, Roosevelt probably under-estimated the extent to which the American people might have been induced to abdicate sovereign rights and assume world responsibility. Where Wilson stubbornly refused to consider modifications of his League Covenant in order to make it acceptable to the United States Senate, Roosevelt preferred to weaken the United Nations Charter rather than run the slightest risk of repudiation. The result was the creation of a world organization readily acceptable to the United States Senate and to the American people but not nearly strong enough to be able to enforce peace.

The American people agreed to enter the United Nations in the widespread belief that, if they did so, they would be assured of enduring peace. When peace failed to materialize they were bitterly disappointed. Those who did not blame Russia blamed the United Nations. And those who saddled the Soviet Union with all the blame were ready to write off the United Nations because Russia "had destroyed its usefulness." Few Americans gave the matter enough serious thought to realize that, in putting their faith in the United Nations as constituted at San Francisco, they had made the mistake of expecting a toy engine to pull a fullsize passenger train. Even when the invention of atomic weapons wholly altered the nature of war and vastly increased the discrepancy between the assignment and the powers given to the United Nations, few Americans attributed its inadequacy to this cause. On the whole, disappointment created an inclination to write off, ignore, or withdraw from the world organization rather than a determination to strengthen it.

This tendency was reflected in the course pursued by the American government. In the postwar period, a succession of American Secretaries of State issued declarations asserting that support of the United Nations must be the corner-stone of American policy. Yet, with few exceptions, the major actions of the United States in the field of foreign affairs were undertaken unilaterally or at least outside of the United Nations. This was due in part to the fact that the United Nations was not charged with *making* but only with *preserving* the peace; and that many of the postwar problems were peace-*making* problems (e.g. Germany) for which the responsibility rested upon the great-power Council of Foreign Ministers.

This limitation upon the jurisdiction of the United Nations does not, however, account for such unilateral American actions as the intervention in Greece, Turkey and China, nor for the failure to channel economic assistance through the United Nations. These actions can be explained only on the ground of dissatisfaction with or lack of confidence in the United Nations machinery, or else on the ground of impatience with consultative processes and an inclination to "go it alone."

Russian obstructionism and abuse of the Security Council veto have, to be sure, provided a rationalization for taking action outside of the United Nations, especially when time has been of the essence. Russian intransigence might, however, just as readily have stimulated a demand for Charter revision. It is significant that, apart from Secretary of State Acheson's initiative in proposing and putting through the "Uniting for Peace Resolution" after the experience gained in the Korean intervention, no such demand for strengthening the United Nations developed as the result of communist obstruction. The trend has been in the opposite direction, toward unilateral action or toward regional defense organizations permitted by the United Nations Charter but scarcely expected by its founders to replace the United Nations as the chief instrument of preserving peace. One might sum up the official United States government attitude toward the United Nations prior to the Egyptian crisis in something like the following paraphrase:

> Soviet obstruction makes it impossible to use the United Nations as more than a forum for discussion. Therefore, other means must be used to prevent aggression. There is no use in discussing a strengthening of the United Nations because the communists would veto any strengthening Charter amendments that might be put forward.

This somewhat defeatist attitude almost certainly did not derive solely from discouragement; it derived at least as much from a reluctance to subordinate American foreign policy to external influence. The widespread support of the Bricker amendment, the coercive tendencies in legislation such as the Battle Act and the overt attacks upon the United Nations and UNESCO by patrioteering groups provide clear evidence that an important segment of American public opinion resents any "outside interference in American pursuit of American objectives."

Were this superpatriotism to become dominant in determining United States foreign policy, it would logically result either in a retreat into neo-isolationism ("Fortress America") or in a reluctant but nevertheless ruthless American imperialism ("The American Century"). As it is, the influence of the isolationist-imperialists has been sufficiently strong to give American policy overtones of arrogance and a tendency toward coercion rather than cooperation.

The Influence of John Foster Dulles

The attitude of Secretary of State Dulles toward the United Nations, which is obviously an important factor in determining the present policy of the United States, can be traced back to the year before the world organization was founded. Mr. Dulles began, in 1944, to represent the Republican Party—more accurately, Governor Thomas E. Dewey—in the inner councils of the Department of State. In that year, he commented as follows upon the draft of the United Nations Charter just formulated at the Dumbarton Oaks Conference:

"The plan to impose peace presupposes a political unity of the great powers which has rarely occurred and which, if it prevails, will itself assure peace. While the Security Council can be useful as a forum where controversial matters are discussed and where public opinion may focus its pressures, the force proposals are little more than scenery."

This was a sharp challenge to President Roosevelt's concept of peace enforcement by the great powers and his declaration that the Security Council "must have the power to act quickly and decisively to keep the peace by force if necessary" and "must be endowed in advance . . . with authority to act."

Mr. Dulles correctly foresaw that the war-time coalition would not last and that the idea of peace enforcement based upon the assumption of great power cooperation was an illusion. From the conviction that the teeth in the proposed Charter would not bite, Mr. Dulles did not, however, draw the conclusion that a better way must be devised to give the new world organization the power to enforce peace. He concluded, on the contrary, that the new world organization should be toothless and that peace enforcement should be left to regional military organizations. Thus, in 1947, Mr. Dulles, then a member of the United States Delegation to the United Nations, recalled his disagreement with President Roosevelt and wrote with smug satisfaction:

"It has not discouraged us to discover that there would not be an indefinitely continuing war alliance to impose peace by force, for we did not believe in that. On the contrary, we redoubled our efforts to make the United Nations a moral mechanism."

In his later book,* Mr. Dulles declared that he personally drafted Article 51 of the United Nations Charter in 1945 at San Francisco, in consultation with the late Senator Vandenberg and Mr. Nelson Rockefeller. (This is the article which permits regional military alliances and under which the United States has sponsored the Organi-

* *War or Peace.* Macmillan, 1950.

zation of American States, the North Atlantic Treaty Organization, the Southeast Asia Treaty Organization, etc.) Mr. Dulles relates in his book how he conceived of the United Nations as a "town meeting of the world" while laboring to develop regional military alliances "within the Charter but outside the veto."

As for the Security Council veto, commonly attributed to Soviet insistence, Mr. Dulles makes it clear that he and the Republicans with whom he worked at San Francisco were convinced that the United States must insist upon the right to veto any enforcement action involving the use of American troops.

Mr. Dulles' actions and pronouncements as Secretary of State supply no indication that his attitude toward the United Nations or toward peace enforcement has changed. His negative attitude toward Charter revision in 1956, was wholly consistent with his earlier work as one of the drafters of the Charter. There has been no indication that President Eisenhower differs from his Secretary of State. The attitude of our government has been to "leave well enough alone."

The Effect of the Egyptian Crisis

With the outbreak of the Egyptian crisis in October, 1956, the attitude of the Eisenhower administration toward the United Nations underwent a sudden change. Faced with the dilemma created by the Anglo-French invasion, the United States government in effect dropped the whole affair into the lap of the United Nations. For a period of two months, it appeared to the world that United Nations Secretary-General Dag Hammarskjold had to all intents and purposes become the foreign minister of the United States. The constructive initiative in creating the United Nations Emergency Force for the Middle East came from Canada's Foreign Secretary, Lester Pearson. Until January 5, 1957, the United States seemed to have no foreign policy other than to support the United Nations in whatever that body might decide to do.

For two months, the American government—dismayed, baffled and uncertain—treated the United Nations as if it were a world government, expecting it to assume responsibilities and to execute tasks which only a world government could be expected to undertake. When the worst of the crisis appeared to have passed, the American government began to take back the responsibilities which it had temporarily abdicated. It did so, however, without giving any indication that it had, through this experience, learned to recognize the need for endowing the United Nations with more adequate powers.

The President's enunciation of the "Eisenhower Doctrine" marked a return swing of the pendulum toward unilateral action. Insofar as it could be considered a declaration of policy, the President's pronouncement meant that the United States had decided to take over from Britain its traditional task of preventing Russian expansion into the Middle East. This intention became more clearly evident in April, 1957, when a crisis broke out in Jordan. The United States promptly declared that it had "a vital interest in Jordan's independence" and dispatched the 6th Fleet to the eastern end of the Mediterranean. The point is not whether this action was effective. The point is that it was unilaterally undertaken.

II
The United States, the United Nations and Disarmament

Throughout a decade of disarmament negotiations, the United States has clearly demonstrated its ambivalent attitude toward the world organization. While professing a desire to achieve universal national disarmament, provided that it could be reliably enforced, the American government has refused to face the fact that there can be no reliable enforcement except by a supranational agency possessing adequate power of its own. The condition precedent to universal disarmament, which no American administration has ever recognized, is the transformation of the United Nations into a world organization capable of enacting, administering and enforcing world law—an organization superior to the nation-states at least to the extent of being endowed with the exclusive right to maintain its own armed force in order to enforce world law upon the disarmed nation-states.

If the American people are not ready—as indeed they are not—to declare their avowed aim to be the establishment of a limited form of world government, then the pursuit of universal disarmament is, for the time being, the pursuit of a mirage. The failure of the American government to recognize this fact has resulted in the miseducation of the American people and has created a situation in which it appears to the world that, while the Russians want disarmament without inspection or enforcement, the United States apparently does not want complete disarmament at all.

Until the United States is prepared to recognize what

adequate enforcement implies in the way of relinquishment of sovereignty, and until the Russians are prepared to accept adequate inspection and enforcement, there can be no hope of universal disarmament. Nor does it make the slightest sense to talk about disarmament so long as China, with one quarter of the world's population, is excluded from the potential enforcement agency.

Living as we do in a time when it is too soon for world government and too late for anything less, the most that we can reasonably hope to accomplish in the immediate future is to arrest the trend toward catastrophe. This we can and must do by halting further tests of nuclear weapons, which endanger the human race even without war, and by taking such practical steps toward disarmament as may be found possible. This is the basic thought underlying a policy of gradual disengagement.

The only presently practical approach to disarmament, apart from the banning of nuclear tests, which can be monitored, is an empirical procedure by which the inspection and enforcement power of the United Nations will be established in gradually widening neutralized belts separating the rival power orbits. One such potential area lies in Europe. Another lies in the Middle East.

The creation of a United Nations Emergency Force in the Middle East has been an important step in this direction. If a permanent base for this force can be established, as suggested in Chapter Six, a pattern may be worked out which can then be applied to other parts of the world.

At present, we are mesmerized by the half-cynical and half-idealistic belief that the modern weapons of mass murder and destruction can save civilization. On the one hand, we believe that the fear of these weapons will prevent war. On the other hand, we assure ourselves that, if war comes, these instruments of annihilation will never be used.

The practical, step-wise approach to disarmament here recommended is admittedly nothing more than a stop-gap procedure by means of which to gain time for mankind to come to its senses.

III
The United States, the United Nations and World Economic Development

Perhaps the greatest opportunities for applying the functional approach to the strengthening of the United Nations lie in the field of world economic development. Here we are dealing not merely with the prevention of war but with the elimination of the causes of war.

In order to explore these possibilities in a study concerned primarily with American foreign policy, it is necessary to review briefly the existing foreign aid program of the United States.

The current American program of foreign aid, known as "Mutual Assistance," involves an annual expenditure of about $4 billion. Roughly 90% of this amount is spent in direct military aid and so-called "defense support" to military allies. Only about $400 *million* is devoted to technical and economic assistance.

The writer questions whether the United States obtains much of a return from its military aid program. NATO, in its present form, is obsolete and has never succeeded in providing an effective shield against Soviet invasion of Western Europe. Weapons and much of the money furnished to France have been used to fight colonial wars.

The huge sums invested in strengthening the Chinese Nationalist regime in Formosa can be considered of value only if our present policy with respect to China is deemed to hold out any promise of establishing peace in the Far East; this, at the very least, is debatable. In the Middle East, it has been proved that arming countries against the danger of Soviet invasion—a danger of which most of them are not aware—merely results in their using the arms so provided to pursue intra-regional disputes and quarrels. Rearming Pakistan has added little if any strength to the anti-communist alliance and has had disastrous political consequences. The only countries where military aid has been undeniably necessary and effective are Turkey, Greece, South Vietnam and the Republic of Korea.

This layman's opinion concerning the value of our military aid program is open to challenge. A fact which cannot be challenged, however, is that military aid to allies, some of which are, to say the least, of dubious value, pre-empts far too great a proportion of the foreign aid program as a whole.

While it is not true that the United States cannot afford to spend more than $400 *million* a year on economic aid so long as it spends over $3.5 *billion* a year on military assistance, this argument has, as a practical matter, stood in the way of the development of an effective foreign economic aid program.

What Can the United States Afford?

Our gross national income is over $400 billion a year. Our government spends about $72 billion, of which over $40 billion goes to national defense. The money we spend

on national defense and military aid to allies achieves no
constructive purpose in eliminating or ameliorating those
conditions of poverty, injustice and oppression which
move men to violence. All that these huge expenditures
can accomplish is to preserve the precarious balance of
terror by which peace is at present being maintained.

The *highest* estimate of what it would take to raise by
2% per annum the income of the peoples living in the
so-called underdeveloped areas of the world, where per
capita income runs from $50 to a maximum of $400 *a
year,* would be about $10 billion per annum. Actually
most experts agree that $3 billion a year is probably about
the maximum that could profitably be put to work at the
present time.

No one would expect the United States to shoulder the
entire burden. In fact, it is essential that the other industrialized countries contribute their share in proportion to
their resources. But, even if the United States were to
provide the entire $3 billion each year, it would be con-
tributing less than the American people spend annually on
cosmetics.

The question is not: "Can we afford to make a contribution of, let us say, $2 billion a year to world economic
development?" The question is: "Can we afford *not* to
make such a contribution?"

There are three major reasons why we cannot afford to
withhold our fair contribution:

First: We have a direct, selfish interest in the development of the underdeveloped areas. Our industries are
becoming more and more dependent upon raw materials
not found within the United States and upon foreign
markets for their expanding production. Our best cus-

tomers are the highly industrialized nations, like Canada and Great Britain. Aid in economic development is the prerequisite for the greater trade which we need in order to maintain our own progress.

Second: We have a direct, selfish interest in eliminating those sources of justified discontent among the impoverished, disease-ridden and undernourished masses of humanity which lead to wars and violent revolutions.

Third; and perhaps most important of all: the dictates of a moral conscience and the belief in the principles of justice and equality upon which this nation was founded demand that we share at least some of our own good fortune with the underprivileged and unhappy majority of the human race.

It is often alleged that the chief reason we must develop a more effective foreign economic aid program is in order to compete successfully with the communist dictatorships. It is true that the Soviet Union is beginning to beat us at our own best game and that this constitutes a very great danger.* But, actually, the communists have created no new imperatives. They have merely shortened the time in which we must do what our own self-interest and our own moral standards have long demanded. Had there been no communist dictatorships, it is possible that the revolt of the underprivileged two-thirds of humanity might have been postponed for another generation. What the communists have done is to force us, here and now, to face the fact that the time is past when the white peoples of the Atlantic Community can hope to live in freedom,

* op. cit. *Danger and Opportunity,* Chapter I. Since this pamphlet was written, the danger has been considerably reduced by the disruption of the Soviet bloc economy through the Polish and Hungarian revolts.

comfort and security, while the rest of the world exists in varying degrees of misery. The communists have merely moved up the dead-line for a decision which had already become inescapable.

Before that dead-line is reached, we shall have to win the confidence and the friendship of the peoples who are emerging into freedom and seeking a fair share of the benefits of the world's productivity, or else our civilization will perish. Before the time left to us expires, we shall have to move into the vanguard of the contemporary world revolution, or else be overrun by it.

Not Only What *We Give But* How *We Give* *Is Important*

This getting into step with the times is by no means solely an economic problem. It involves not only material aid but other factors, such as the graceful liquidation of colonialism and the dissipation of the idea of white supremacy. It involves not only how much we give or lend but, even more, *how* we give or lend assistance.

Quite a few of the so-called underdeveloped countries have ancient cultures and a history far longer than our own. For the most part, these countries can be called backward or underdeveloped only in the economic sense. This is especially true of the crucially important subcontinent of India.

The problem is not solely one of providing technical advice and capital assistance. What is needed, first of all, is a true, empathetic understanding on the part of those who wish to assist these peoples to catch up to the mid-twentieth century.

Empathy is quite a different thing from sympathy. Sympathy means sharing and, to a certain extent, agreeing with the feelings of others. Empathy means entering into another's state of mind and feeling, without necessarily agreeing with it. Sympathy requires merely an emotional identification, often based upon subjective factors rather than upon true understanding. Empathy requires a depth of understanding attainable only through the ability to project oneself fully into the skin of another human being.

We, the American people, are long on sympathy, but we are woefully short of the ability to project ourselves into the mental and emotional state of peoples living in distant lands and in circumstances radically different from those to which we are accustomed. We are abysmally ignorant of languages, cultures, religions and historical backgrounds other than our own. Thus, with all our sympathy, our good intentions and our abundant resources, we are ill-equipped to render the help we desire to extend.

Our shortcomings in this respect are by no means unique. Nations with far more extensive experience than ours in dealing with other peoples, such as, for example the European colonial powers, have often shown themselves curiously obtuse in understanding the psychology of those whom they call "the natives." What is more, they have frequently abused what understanding they possessed in order to exploit and oppress, rather than to assist and liberate.

True understanding of one people by another exists, broadly speaking, only within certain cultural families. The West Europeans, for example, thoroughly understand even when they do not like each other. The Indians understand the Burmese. The Arabs, disunited and torn though they are by dissension, understand each other. But it is scarcely necessary to point out how little understanding exists between the Arabs and the peoples of the West, or between Europe and Asia, or between us and any of the non-English speaking peoples.

The Need for Collective Judgment

The point of all this is that the empathetic understanding essential to helpful cooperation exists only collectively. No one nation, least of all the United States, knows enough about all the peoples of the underdeveloped areas to render them effective assistance, because assistance, to be effective, must be rendered in terms of helping a recipient people to realize its own aims in its own way, irrespective of whether those aims or means coincide or correspond with the ideas of those who render the assistance.

To say this is not to say that the countries in need of aid should be given whatever they ask or desire. Obviously, sound judgment must be applied to conserve the available resources.* The point is that only a collective judgment can in most cases be expected to produce constructive results.

Where Can a Collective Judgment Be Formed?

The answer to this question should, of course, be: in the United Nations. But here we encounter a serious obstacle.

The history of the development of the United Nations during the first decade of its existence is marked by the

* For an excellent study of the criteria to be applied see M. F. Millikan and W. W. Rostow—*A Proposal, Key to an Effective Foreign Policy,* Harper, 1956.

unanticipated weakness of its quasi-executive organs and the consequent strengthening of the General Assembly.

The Security Council has been paralyzed by abuse of the veto. The Economic and Social Council has become impotent because its deliberations and debates, conducted by relatively low-level representatives, are usually repeated by higher-level representatives in the General Assembly.

At the same time, the nature of the Assembly has been considerably altered by the admission of new members. While in itself a desirable development, since the United Nations was conceived as a universal organization, the admission of new members has radically altered the balance of voting power.

Broadly speaking, the balance of power in the original Assembly lay in the hands of the relatively more developed and wealthier countries of the North Atlantic community. It has now shifted toward the relatively underdeveloped and poorer nations of Asia, Africa and the Middle East with whom some of the Latin American republics have tended more and more to ally themselves.

The problem which thus arises is that of an imbalance between the nations which will have to supply the greater part of the funds with which the United Nations must be endowed, if it is to realize its maximum potential of usefulness, and the Assembly majority consisting of nations which will presumably be the beneficiaries of economic assistance. This accounts in large measure for the present reluctance of the wealthier nations to channel their economic aid through the world organization. It accounts for our government's unwillingness to contribute to the plan for a Special United Nations Fund for Economic Development (SUNFED), put forward three years ago by some of the non-industrialized nations.

IV
A Proposal for A United Nations Development Authority*

The writer's suggestion for solving this problem would be to create a United Nations Development Authority, so constituted as to give appropriate representation both to the nations supplying it with funds and to those seeking assistance. This could be done without Charter revision by a two-thirds vote of the Assembly, which might conceivably be accompanied by a decision to abolish the Economic and Social Council, except for its Commission on Human Rights.

The Development Authority might be constituted somewhat along the lines of the Security Council, except that there would be no veto. Five permanent seats might be allotted to the industrialized nations as a whole, to be occupied each year by those particular industrialized nations which in the preceding year had made the largest contributions of funds. Another five or six seats would be occupied by rotating regional representatives of the non-industrialized beneficiary nations.

In addition to the parent body, there would be created regional subsidiaries, such as the Middle East Development Authority discussed in Chapter Six. Each of these regional boards would sift the problems and opportunities existing in its area and assign priorities to the specific projects of which it approved. Each regional board would

* The essence of this proposal was put forward in a paper presented before the League for Industrial Democracy in New York City on April 13, 1957.

then, through its annually rotating spokesman on the parent body, present its approved projects for consideration.

The fixing of priorities among the projects recommended by the various regional boards, as well as the actual allocation of funds, would be determined by the parent body in which the industrialized nations occupying the permanent seats would exercise the decisive influence. A majority of the five nations holding these seats would be required for the approval of any appropriation.

Thus the ultimate control of the funds would rest with the United States and the four other major contributors of which the Soviet Union would undoubtedly be one, if it elected to participate in the scheme. However, the Soviet Union alone could not obstruct action, since there would be no veto; nor could it, in the foreseeable future, control a majority as against the Western industrialized nations, since none of its satellites would be likely to become major contributors. Even if the Chinese People's Republic were to become a member of the United Nations and to earn the right to a seat on the Development Authority as a major contributor, there would be only two communist votes out of five.

This raises the question whether the communist dictatorships—specifically, the Soviet Union—would agree to cooperate in any such proposal. We do not know, because no such proposal has been advanced. The Soviet note of February 12, 1957, concerning economic assistance to the Middle East* certainly does not rule out the possibility of Soviet cooperation. Should the proposal be put forward and should the Kremlin agree to it, then one

* Essential portion quoted on pages 134-135 of Chapter Six.

of the major facets of the cold war would be eliminated. If, on the other hand, the Western Powers were to make the proposal and the Kremlin rejected it, it is more than likely that the United Nations General Assembly would approve the project by a two-thirds vote in spite of Soviet objection. Should the Kremlin succeed in blocking Assembly approval or, failing in that effort, decline to participate in the Development Authority, the Soviet Union would lose much of its influence upon the mostly unaligned peoples of the underdeveloped areas.

Advantages to be Gained

What would be the advantage of such a multinational approach, as opposed to the binational method by which we have been trying to solve the problem?

1. A United Nations Development Authority with regional subsidiaries would be better equipped than the bureaucratic or legislative machinery of any one nation to understand and evaluate relative needs for assistance and to determine how and upon what conditions assistance should be rendered.

2. Conditions imposed by a United Nations Development Authority would be more readily accepted by beneficiary governments and peoples than would the same conditions, if imposed by any single nation. This would be especially important where such conditions might involve fiscal reform, or land reform, or the creation of credit facilities to displace firmly entrenched, usurious money-lenders. In many countries these reforms are fundamental to progress.

3. Economic development requires planning for several years ahead and the assurance that capital for ap-

proved plans will be available. A United Nations Development Authority could more readily make long-range plans and long range commitments than can most national government, especially our own. This would be true even if the Congress were to approve the proposal for a mechanism permitting long-range commitments put forward by Secretary Dulles on April 8, 1957.

4. To the extent that all contributing nations, including the Soviet Union, could be induced to channel their contributions through the United Nations Development Authority, aid to worldwide economic development would be stripped of the overtones of competitive power politics.

The Growing Sentiment for Such a Proposal

There is nothing original about the foregoing proposal except its precise formulation. The need for some sort of instrument by means of which economic aid might be internationalized has long been recognized, except in the United States and the Soviet Union. Asian leaders, among them Prime Minister Nehru of India, have for years advocated a multilateral approach. Great Britain and the Commonwealth countries have developed the regional Colombo Plan. Mr. David Owen, head of the United Nations Technical Assistance Board, reported in April, 1956, after a tour of Asian countries, that the leaders in these countries had "underlined over and over again the importance of an international, multilateral approach." At the meeting of the NATO Council, in May, 1956, French Foreign Minister Pineau called for the creation of "an agency for world economic development responsible to the United Nations," urging that NATO members should join in supporting this project in the United Nations. Nothing came of this proposal, chiefly because it was cold-shouldered by the American Secretary of State.

The attitude of Mr. Dulles on this occasion was somewhat surprising since, just prior to the Secretary's departure for Paris, the United States chief delegate to the United Nations, Henry Cabot Lodge Jr., had stated that in his judgment the world situation demanded that the United States channel a larger share of its foreign aid through the United Nations. The apparent disharmony within the American administration caused considerable comment. In response to a press conference question, President Eisenhower declared, on May 11, 1956, that he did not think the United States "could surrender control of its foreign expenditures to an international body." *

The objection to handing over control of substantial sums of money to an international agency is not wholly rational. The rational objections would be met by the proposal here submitted. The irrational components of opposition to any such idea can be overcome only by the same patient processes which are required to defeat such ultra-nationalist proposals as the Bricker Amendment.

The angry question: "If we put up the money, haven't we the right to say how every penny of it should be spent?" can best be answered by saying: "Certainly we have the right. The question is only whether we shall be wise—wise in our own self-interest—to insist upon it."

* *New York Times,* May 12, 1956.

NINE

PRIVATE INVESTMENT AND

INTERNATIONAL TRADE

Foreign aid is only one part of that policy which determines the economic relations of the United States to the rest of the world. The other two parts are private investment and foreign trade policy.

Economic assistance has been discussed in the preceding chapter because of its obvious connection with the relationship between the United States and the United Nations. The other two parts of foreign economic policy are equally important.

The whole of foreign economic policy became a major subject of discussion during the 1956 session of the 84th Congress, after it became apparent that the Soviet economic offensive posed a serious threat to American supremacy. There were many speeches and long debates, but the only concrete result of this discussion was to authorize the expenditure of a considerable sum of the taxpayers' money in procuring a multitude of reports by committees, subcommittees, commissions and private advisory groups. These reports concerned themselves almost entirely with foreign aid. A few were excellent. Others cancelled each other out with conflicting advice. Almost none touched upon foreign trade policy and only a few raised the question of private investment.

Can Private Capital Do The Job?

One rather significant report emphasized private investment chiefly in order to show the absence of any need for a governmental foreign aid policy. The American Enterprise Association, of which Mr. John B. Hollister, director of the government's foreign aid programs, is a trustee, declared: "Private investment, not government aid, is the most effective way of helping other peoples to improve their levels of living."

The widespread belief here expressed has greatly contributed to the inadequacy of our foreign aid programs. One of the favorite arguments of those who oppose all foreign aid is that loans from the World Bank (International Bank for Reconstruction and Development) or the Export-Import Bank, plus private investment, are sufficient to lift the living standards of the depressed areas.

The simple fact is that neither bank loans nor private investment can possibly supply the funds needed for malaria and pest control, for irrigation and flood control, for harbor and transportation development, for the building of schools and hospitals, or for the training of doctors, nurses, teachers and administrative officials.

World Bank and Export-Import Bank loans can be made only within the strict limits of charter requirements, demanding, in the one case, assurances of repayment and, in the other, promotion of American exports. So far as its limited capital of $100 million permits, the International Finance Corporation will be able to broaden the field a little, but the amount of its available resources is insignificant in relation to the need. To say this is not to belittle the extremely useful function fulfilled by these lending institutions but only to emphasize the limited area of their operations.

As for private investment, the *ten-year total* of American private investment in the underdeveloped areas, apart from the exploitation of mineral resources, amounted in 1955 to only about $100 *million*. During the same ten-year period private investment within the United States averaged over *$45 billion each year*. The reason is obvious. Private capital seeks maximum profit at minimum risk. But there is plenty of risk and no profit in undertaking the first steps necessary to lift the living standards of the depressed areas. Before private investors will venture into the underdeveloped areas to any substantial extent—except to extract natural resources—seed-money out of public funds must create the economic conditions which will attract private venture capital; and diplomatic effort must create a favorable political context. Even then, private capital will not always be welcome because it has for so long been associated in the minds of dependent or formerly dependent peoples with colonial rule and foreign exploitation.

Quite apart from these considerations, the statement of the American Enterprise Association overlooks the very important fact that the world's capital market was destroyed in 1931-1932 and that it has never been re-established. It is perfectly true that prior to the Great Depression the development of what were then called the backward areas was financed chiefly by private or semi-private investment. In those days, the governments of the industrialized countries had not resorted to exchange controls and restrictions upon the export of capital. The vicious circle of autarchy had not yet developed. Capital could and did move freely into areas where a greater risk was compensated by higher interest rates and greater opportunities for profit. There was then no serious threat of expropriation by the governments of the underdeveloped areas and no serious question of the transferability of profits and return of capital.

It may well be that in some respects this was a more natural way to promote worldwide economic development, but it must not be overlooked that under this system the backward areas were developed more for the profit of the developers than for the benefit of the peoples concerned. Whatever the merits of the old system, it is idle to talk about letting private capital do the job until an international capital market is restored.

The restoration of a capital market depends, more than upon any other single factor, upon the foreign trade policies pursued by the wealthier, more industrialized nations.

Foreign Trade Policy—Pressures for Protection

Most thinking Americans realize that it is essential for continued American prosperity that the exchange of goods and services among nations should be freed to the greatest extent possible from artificial barriers and restrictions. In this sense, most thinking Americans are in principle "free traders." Actually, they are free traders only up to the point at which their own special interests become involved.

At this point most of them become ardent protectionists.

The fact is that the United States could do as much, if not more, for world economic development by liberalizing its tariff policy as it could by even the most generous program of foreign loans, grants and investments. It is certainly true that the effectiveness of a more liberal and more wisely conceived foreign aid program would be severely limited by continued failure to open the American market more generously to the goods produced in other countries. As for private American investment abroad, this will remain only a theoretical possibility unless foreign countries are enabled to earn the dollars with which to return profits and repay capital.

It is not necessary to restate here the familiar case demonstrating that a more liberal import policy is in the interest of the American people as a whole. We all know that our prosperity depends upon expanding exports. We all know that we cannot continue to increase our exports unless we increase our imports. We all know that it would benefit not only our export industries but the American consumer if goods that can be made more cheaply abroad were permitted to enter the American market. We all know that it would be in the national interest—although temporarily painful to certain sectors of our economy—if certain high-cost American producers now protected by the tariff were forced to direct their productive energies into other fields in which they could successfully compete with foreign manufacturers. We all know that it would be quite possible to cushion the necessary readjustments by government action.

We know all these things—but when our own ox is gored, we forget all about the national interest. Labor unions are every bit as bad as high-cost manufacturers. Labor leaders clamor for protection against "cheap foreign labor," forgetting that the low productivity of foreign labor is often more significant than its low wage-level. High-cost manufacturers take refuge in claiming that their businesses are essential to national defense. Farmers—and this is true throughout most of the Western world—claim a right to protection against having to sell their crops at world prices. The agricultural policies of the Western world, instead of being aimed at making more food available to more people at lower prices, operate so as to price the consumer out of the market and to accumulate huge, costly surpluses while two-thirds of the world's population remains undernourished.

The United States is not the only sinner by any means. The industrialized countries of Western Europe, broadly speaking, pursue much the same protectionist policies. The European governments are no less subject to the pushing and hauling of special interest pressure groups than the government of the United States.

But the United States is the worst sinner, because, more than any other nation, the United States could afford to lead the way toward a liberalization of international trade and international capital investment.

It is only fair to say that the government of the United States has made considerable efforts in this direction. Under the Reciprocal Trade Treaties Act of 1934 and its extensions, American import restrictions have been substantially lowered over the past twenty years. More than any other Republican President, Mr. Eisenhower has at least verbally supported a liberal foreign trade policy, even though he has been strangely reluctant to fight for it.

But the American effort has, ever since its inception under President Roosevelt, suffered from a basic defect; it has failed to make a distinction between industrialized nations and nations seeking to catch up to the industrial revolution.

The American effort, through the General Agreements on Tariffs and Trade (GATT) and the projected Organization for Trade Cooperation, has been directed toward the adoption *by all nations* of certain uniform principles. This overlooks the fact that equal treatment is equitable only among equals. It fails to make provision for the legitimate needs of the young, not yet industrialized nations for protection—the same type of protectionism which was needed by our own infant industries when the United States, too, was an underdeveloped country. The need is for what Mr. Gunnar Myrdal has called "a double standard" of trade morality—one standard for the industrialized nations and the other for those emerging into the industrial era. This our Government has not recognized.

Quite apart from this basic defect in the aim of American foreign trade policy, the recent trend has been discouraging. More and more use is being made of escape clauses to frustrate tariff reduction. Congress has become increasingly reluctant to renew the Reciprocal Trade Treaties Act and, at each successive renewal, has weakened it. American membership in the American-sponsored Organization for Trade Cooperation is powerfully opposed and only half-heartedly advocated. The "Buy American Act" is still on the books. The formerly free-trade agricultural South is becoming industrialized and protectionist.

Worst of all, the whole question of foreign trade policy

is scarcely discussed, except by those directly interested. Yet it cannot be emphasized too strongly that no amount of generosity in foreign economic aid and no amount of humanitarian interest in the welfare of the world's underprivileged peoples will produce much of a result until the American people as a whole assert the interest of the nation as a whole in overcoming protectionist pressures.

Summary

The five imperatives for an American foreign economic policy adequate to meet the needs of the existing world situation are:

1. To re-examine the efficacy of the military assistance programs and, in any case, to separate them from economic aid to world development. (The separation was at long last recommended by Secretary Dulles on April 8, 1957.)

2. To recognize that the United States can well afford to make available for world economic development a sum of $2-$3 billion a year, which is more than will be necessary if other industrialized nations do their part.

3. To shift the emphasis from bilateral to multilateral administration of economic assistance, preferably through a strengthened United Nations.

4. To discard the false notion that bank loans and private investment can supply the funds needed for world development.

5. To revise and liberalize American foreign trade policy.

The prospects for action along these lines are not bright. A President, reluctant to advocate what he conceives to be unpopular action, has recommended little more than a continuation of the present, wholly inadequate programs. A Congress, anxious to economize and to lower taxes without reducing any expenditures affecting domestic pressure groups, inclines toward reducing rather than increasing foreign aid. Protectionist lobbies dominate consideration of tariff policy.

Yet five public opinion polls, conducted for the White House in 1957 by the National Opinion Research Center at the University of Chicago, showed that 71% of the American people considered economic aid more important than military assistance, and that 52% thought that economic aid should be given to countries, like India, which have not associated themselves with the United States as military allies.

These opinion tests seemed to indicate that both the Eisenhower administration and the Democratic-controlled Congress underestimated the potential public support for an enlarged and revised program of economic assistance. The people, it seemed, were ahead of their government . . .

But, were they really? Did the fault lie solely or even mostly in Washington?

What would have been the response of the people, had they been asked: "Which do you consider more important, an expanded program of foreign economic aid or a tax cut?"

THE CITIZEN'S
RESPONSIBILITY FOR
WORLD LEADERSHIP

No one, whether Republican or Democrat, can claim that American postwar policy has been a success. If the aim of American postwar policy has been to halt communist expansion, communist expansion has not been halted. If our aim has been to unite the non-communist world, it has not been united. And if our overall objective has been the firm establishment of peace, it must be admitted that we are no nearer to peace than we were ten years ago.

Opinions may and do differ as to how much of an overall failure our postwar policy has been; and also as to how much of that failure could have been prevented. It still remains true that we have neither reached nor made any great progress toward reaching our basic objectives.

Having discussed some of the shortcomings of our

government, it seems appropriate at this point to explore
those reasons for our failure which may properly be said
to have their roots in the nature of the American society
—that is to say, in us collectively as responsible (or ir-
responsible) citizens of the United States.

Ignorance and Indifference

Looking at the matter from this point of view, one is
inclined to suggest that the most obvious cause contributing to our nation's failure as a world leader is ignorance
—ignorance of geography, ignorance of languages and
cultures other than our own and, above all, ignorance of
history.

We are constantly learning too late. We begin to acquire rudimentary knowledge of the geography of an area
such as southeast Asia or the Middle East only when a
crisis has arisen sufficiently serious to cause sketch-maps
to accompany the front-page stories in our newspapers.
Thus, we began to learn geography during the war; and,
since the war, we have discovered the existence and the
whereabouts of places in Asia like Jakarta, Pusan, Ban-
dung and Saigon, or Damascus, Elath, Amman and
Riyadh in the Middle East. By the time we know something about the geography of an area—not to mention
its history—it is quite likely to have been lost to hostile
influence.

We learn languages—if we learn them at all—through
vacation travel or business connections. We learn them
in order to buy meals or trinkets, or to engage in profit-
able transactions, but not in order to understand the culture and literature of other peoples. That sort of language
study we leave to the so-called experts. But, when we

suddenly desire to establish an effective propaganda service in the Middle East, we find that an American who can speak fluent Arabic is as rare as a Sanskrit scholar.

Our knowledge of history is incredibly parochial and, even as such, limited. To all intents and purposes, history begins for the average American citizen with the settlement of Jamestown and the landing of the Pilgrim Fathers at Plymouth Rock. The French and Indian Wars are vaguely recorded in our minds without any comprehension of their European context. The War of 1812 has no relation to the Napoleonic Wars. We are familiar with the American Revolution and amazingly well-informed and fascinated by our Civil War. But to most Americans World War I consists of the *Lusitania,* "Hang the Kaiser," Belleau Wood and Chateau Thierry; while World War II begins with Pearl Harbor and ends with the Battle of the Bulge, Hiroshima and the Japanese surrender on board the battleship *Missouri.* About the developments in times of peace which have caused or could cause wars and battles, the average American knows but little.

Why are we so ignorant of the past and so unfamiliar with the world beyond our own border? Obviously, one reason is that we have until recently lived in a more or less self-sufficient little world of our own. But a whole generation of Americans has grown up since this secluded, nursery-like, happy existence became a memory. Most Americans now living knew, even when they were children at school, that the United States had become a world power and that the American destiny was inextricably interwoven with that of many other peoples in distant lands. To say that most Americans know this is, of course, not to say that they have accepted it. But why has this generation of Americans not come to terms with what it knows to be a fact? Why has it not sought to inform itself?

In part, the fault lies, one must suppose, with an educational system that overemphasizes the natural sciences and vocational training, neglecting philosophy and the social sciences, especially history. But this does not explain why the majority of Americans are satisfied with such a system of education. It does not explain the absence of a popular demand for better teaching of languages, geography, history and the social sciences.

The media of mass communication could, no doubt, cater less to the prevalent taste for sensation and entertainment and perform more of an educational function than they do. But, again, this does not explain the existence of the prevalent taste.

The simple fact is that we are not ignorant about the world in which we live because the facts are unavailable to us. In terms of what is available, we should be the best informed people in the world. We are ignorant, not because knowledge is beyond our reach, but because we are not interested enough to reach for it. Our ignorance is an expression of a curious indifference.

Alienation

This raises the much more difficult question of why Americans should be indifferent to matters which directly and vitally concern the safety and survival of their families, their homes, their businesses, their jobs—in other words, the whole "way of life" which they cherish and wish to preserve. The writer would like to suggest certain lines of inquiry which might prove fruitful.

To a very large extent, the indifference to world affairs and to the formation of national policy may be due to a sense of impotence and frustration. The average citizen of the United States has become more and more alienated from the democratic processes of decision-making. The problems of national policy seem to him too complicated for his comprehension. The decision-makers seem too remote for him to be able to exercise any influence. We are no longer a nation of small farmers and small businessmen, each accustomed to weighing certain familiar risks and making decisions. We have become a nation of wage and salary earners, dependent for our livelihoods upon Big Business or Big Government. Our daily lives no longer demand the weighing of risks and the taking of decisions. The risks are weighed and the decisions taken for us by the managers of Big Business and Big Government. This may be one factor causing apparent apathy. If so, it would seem important to seek ways and means by which the average citizen's sense of proprietary interest in and responsibility for national policy may be restored, so that the democratic process may function in a modern mass society.

Perversion of Bipartisanship

A second line of investigation might lead us to inquire why we make so little use of the opportunities for public education presented by an election year. In the past three Presidential elections, we have had practically no informative discussion of foreign policy. We have had what amounted to a bipartisan conspiracy of silence. Insofar as foreign policy and world affairs were mentioned at all, they were discussed in terms of hindsight partisan criticism or defense, without reference or relevance to future courses of action.

In our most recent election campaign, the leaders of both parties avoided any serious discussion of world affairs. As one politician put it, "There is no mileage in discussing foreign policy," meaning that the American people would be bored by any such discussion. It is doubtless true that the people were bored by the Polly-anna propaganda of an administration that boasted of having established peace and by the Cassandra-like croakings of an opposition which denied the administration's extravagant claims and decried its doings but offered few alternatives to the policies it criticized. Given the choice between soothing syrup and castor oil, the people preferred the more pleasant medicine, in spite of the fact that, as election day approached, the evidence accumulated that all was not exactly well in the best of all possible worlds. But this does not prove that the people would not have been interested in an informative discussion during which existing policies and possible alternatives would have been debated on their merits. The people have always shown themselves interested in any issue over which the candidates seriously lock horns in an election year.

To say this is not to suggest that Mr. Adlai Stevenson would have been elected, if he had chosen to make foreign policy a major issue, although he might well have been elected, if he had laid the groundwork for a dissenting position during the four years between elections. The point is that the function of the opposition in a two-party system is to ventilate the defects of existing policies and to propose the means of remedying them. This applies to opposition leadership in the Congress no less than to opposition candidates for the Presidency. Fortunately, some of the opposition leaders in the Congress at last began to fullfil this function in 1957.

The concept of bipartisanship in foreign policy has become dangerously perverted. Granted that, in times of crisis, united support of our nation's foreign policy is desirable, such support is useful and constructive only if all the aspects of foreign policy have first been hammered out in full and free debate between the party in power and the opposition. When bipartisanship merely provides an excuse for indolence and a cloak for timid conformity, it actually endangers the nation's security by depriving national policy of informed public support. "Don't rock the boat" is a poor slogan when the boat is headed for the rocks.

In addition to ignorance and apparent indifference, there are a number of other characteristics of *homo Americanus* which seem worthy of investigation.

Attitude Toward Power

One of the obstacles to our nation's emergence as an effective world leader is a limited concept of power and a curious attitude toward its acquisition and use. It appears to be inherent in the American character to seek power with considerable energy and determination and then, having attained it, not to have any very clear notion of how to put it to use. One might call this an almost purposeless acquisitiveness—a pursuit of power more because of a keen competitive instinct than because of any wish to possess and exercise it.

What is more, we seem unable to distinguish between

different kinds of power and their uses. We seem to
associate the use of power with coercion, although there
are many ways of using various kinds of power to gain
freely given consent and cooperation. This may be a
symptom of an American culture which grew out of a
frontier society. In any case, one suspects that our invention and possession of atomic weapons and our government's excessive preoccupation with military policy have
increased the tendency to think of all power as physical
power and, hence, to regard its use as morally reprehensible, except in self-defense. Whatever the origin of this
rather limited concept of power, its prevalence inhibits
the full development of precisely those non-physical and
non-coercive components of national influence and power
which are essential to leadership, especially in an age
in which force has lost its force as an instrument of national policy.

Generosity and Niggardliness

Closely linked to this ambiguous attitude toward power
is our somewhat similar attitude toward the private and
public expenditure of money. As individuals, we are a
free-spending and generously giving people. As citizens
—that is to say, as taxpayers—we are extremely tight-
fisted. In principle, we want our nation to reflect in its
actions the same generosity toward other peoples which
we express as individuals when we contribute unstintingly
to the relief of suffering throughout the world. But, in
practice, we are most reluctant to permit the use of public
funds for such purposes. As a result, our government em-
barks upon bold new programs of aid to worldwide economic development, such as no other nation has ever

undertaken, only to have its projects all too frequently emasculated by niggardly appropriations. Thus we raise false hopes and cause bitter disappointment. Without attempting to explain this phenomenon, which also possibly bears some relation to the somewhat anarchic attitude of a pioneer society toward all governmental authority, the writer submits that this habit of mind inhibits the development of effective American leadership.

Self-Righteousness

We come now to a somewhat delicate subject. Bluntly stated, it is this observer's belief that our failure to realize our potential leadership is due in large measure to the fact that we not only moralize too much and confuse legalism with morality, but that we often exhibit a self-righteousness which cannot fail to be obnoxious to other peoples.

Let it be clear that the writer does not agree with that school of thought which holds that moral standards cannot be applied to the conduct of nations. If one accepts the doctrine that the sole obligation of a national government is to pursue what it deems to be "the national interest," one ends up by endorsing the Bismarckian thesis that might makes right. Most Americans rightly reject that thesis, holding that, while nations cannot be judged precisely by the standards applied to individuals, certain moral criteria do properly apply to national conduct.

Our trouble is that we confuse moral criteria with legalism, and that our legalism is often based upon incorrect assumptions as to the existing body of law. Our government's recent actions with respect to the Middle East illustrate both tendencies.

But our failure to recognize the inadequacy of treaties as law enforceable by due process and our failure to distinguish between technical and moral judgments is, unfortunately, not our only shortcoming in this area. Our leadership potential suffers even more from the all too frequent assumption that we possess infallible knowledge of what is right and what is wrong. The utterances of our present Secretary of State sometimes give the impression that he is in constant and direct communication with the Deity. Although the average American citizen may not carry self-righteousness to quite that sanctimonious extreme, it is, nevertheless, a national characteristic to view the world in terms of black and white and according to a moral standard which Americans blandly assume to be universally accepted. Once during an earlier Arab-Israeli dispute a well-intentioned assistant to the American mediator exclaimed without any awareness of the absurdity of what he was saying: "Come, come gentlemen. Let us all calm down and look at this thing like good Christians!"

To sharpen the last two points:

We cannot exercise effective leadership so long as we act as if there were a body of enforceable supranational law, when no such body of law exists and when the so-called laws that do exist are unenforceable. We do the United Nations a disservice by treating it as if it were a world government. The alternative is to dedicate ourselves openly to the transformation of the United Nations into an organization that can enact world law and enforce it, meanwhile recognizing its limitations.

We cannot exercise effective leadership until we recognize that, just as there are a number of religions in the world, so also there are codes of moral behavior which do not necessarily conform to our standards of right and wrong. We have both a right and a duty to live up to our idea of what a universal moral standard should be. But we must learn to respect the moral judgments of others even when we disagree with them. If there is one quality more essential to leadership in this age than any other, it is true humility.

Finally, world leadership accrues to a nation only when the spirit of leadership is in its people; that is to say, when the nature and behavior of a people are such as to exercise a power of attraction and to inspire the friendship and emulation of other peoples.

Leadership accrued to ancient Greece not because of the conquests of Alexander but because of the emulation inspired by the Age of Pericles. Leadership accrued to Rome, not because of Caesar's conquests, but because Rome inspired even in barbarians the desire to become Roman citizens. In its history to date, our own country came nearest to real world leadership in the days when Thomas Jefferson wrote the Declaration of Independence. In those days we had no physical power comparable to that of Britain, France and Spain. But we had the power of a revolutionary idea—the idea that governments derive their powers from the consent of the governed and that they exist to serve the dignity and the full development of individual man in his enjoyment of life, liberty and the pursuit of happiness.

We shall not achieve world leadership—we shall not be worthy of achieving world leadership—until we rub the rust from the beliefs upon which this nation was founded—until we revitalize the meaning of the American Revolution.

World leadership cannot be won on the potential bat-
tlefields between us and the communist dictatorships. It
must be won primarily here at home. Montgomery, Alabama, is today a more crucial point in this respect than
Budapest, Cairo or Jerusalem.

To say all this is not to condone the shortcomings of
those men to whom the American people have entrusted
the making of foreign policy during recent years. We, as
citizens, cannot be held responsible for the tactical blunders of an inept Secretary of State nor for the reluctance
of a President to exercise firm leadership. But we are
responsible at least in part for the static inflexibility of
our nation's foreign policy in a rapidly changing world.
We are responsible for a climate of opinion in which any
radical change of course is viewed as a confession of
error rather than as an adjustment to altered circumstance.

It seems quite likely, for example, that both President
Eisenhower and Secretary Dulles might, if left to their
own devices, alter our present policy with respect to
China, knowing that policy to be dangerous, self-defeat-
ing and divisive of the anti-communist coalition. Yet the
President and the Secretary of State have become so
much the prisoners of a public state of mind, created
largely by their own propaganda, that, to date, they have
not dared to make any change. Many leading Democrats,
among them the most recent Democratic candidate for
the Presidency, must be equally aware of the fact that we
are in a dead-end street in the Far East and yet have
been equally unwilling to recommend a revision of our
policy.

The inflexibility and, hence, the unimaginativeness of
our foreign policy—and these are, in this observer's opin-

ion, its greatest shortcomings—result in large measure from the unwillingness of popular leaders to risk their popularity by advocating or doing unpopular things. This hoarding of popularity, instead of putting it to use, is a serious defect of leadership. But the fact remains that the things which need to be done—the adjustments to changing circumstance which need to be made—are unpopular. They are unpopular because the people of the United States, lacking leadership direction for their humanitarian and creative impulses, have been living in a state of ignorance, indifference and smug self-satisfaction—living as if nothing much mattered except new cars, new houses, new clothes, new gadgets and lower taxes.

This does not excuse the default of leadership and the almost deliberate creation by leadership of such a sterile climate of opinion. But neither does it exculpate us, as citizens, from preferring pleasant bedtime stories to the truth.

Least of all does it excuse those of us who work in the field of political and social science from failure to direct public attention to the possibilities for creative action which lie before us. We are so bogged down in contemplation of the dangers of this dangerous age that we fail to realize that its perils and problems are dwarfed by its vast, unexplored opportunities.

The challenge which confronts all of us is to become informed and responsible citizens not only of the United States but of the world. We belong to that small minority of the human race which has for several centuries dominated the course of world history, chiefly by reason of its superiority in technological progress. That period in which Western Man ruled supreme has ended. It has ended chiefly because Western Man has been selfishly acquisitive, because he has failed to live up to the moral principles in which he professed belief, and because the Western peoples have wasted their powers in fratricidal conflict.

Neither we nor any of the other denizens of the North Atlantic Basin can survive merely by composing our differences and forming a united front against the rest of the world. We can survive only by learning to live humbly in and with a world which has passed forever out of our domination and control.

We of the West must get out of military uniform, if we hope to exercise any influence upon a world hungry for peace. If we are to work successfully together in adjusting ourselves to changed and rapidly changing circumstances, a military alliance is not an appropriate embodiment of our solidarity. A Western military alliance may be temporarily required for necessary defense. It may even have some virtue insofar as it may serve to demonstrate to the world that the long-quarreling nations of the West have at long last learned to live together in peace. A non-military political alliance would better serve this purpose. But even such an alliance of the Western peoples will hold no great hope for the future, if it is organized as an association of predominantly white-populated and relatively prosperous nations concerned primarily with preserving as much as possible of the *status quo*.

It is infinitely more important for the Western nations to cultivate friendships among the non-Western peoples than to band together as a separate part of the human race.

Our future—the future of Western Man—will be determined by our ability to guide and to aid rather than to resist inevitable change—by our creative vision and inventive skill, rather than by our physical power—by the strength of our example, rather than by our preachments.

As citizens of the United States, we face the task of making the vision of our forefathers come true—of completing the arrested American Revolution.

As citizens of the world, limitless opportunities lie before us—far greater opportunities than any Americans have enjoyed since our ancestors opened up a new continent.

What we, as individuals, can do is to cease being parochial-minded, passive passengers, becoming, instead, active informed participants in the greatest adventure yet entered upon by the human race. That adventure is nothing less than the final realization of an ancient vision—the vision of the brotherhood of man.

Men have dreamed throughout the centuries of a world in which all nations, all races and all peoples would be united in a common purpose. What was once a dream has now become the imperative of survival.

Could there be a challenge more worthy of the effort of each and every member of the human race? Is there a people on this earth so richly endowed by history to meet this challenge as the people of the United States?

ELEVEN

A POST-SCRIPT

TO THE YOUNGER GENERATION

*(From a Commencement Address
delivered at Roosevelt University in Chicago,
on June 10, 1957)*

According to tradition, a commencement speaker is expected to offer sage advice to a rising generation. Out of the presumed wisdom of his presumed maturity, he is supposed to distill sound precepts for the achievement of success and attractively palatable prescriptions for the attainment of happiness.

I cannot in good conscience attempt anything of the sort.

In the first place, I am not at all sure that I know what success is, or that it is necessarily a wholly desirable objective. One of my oldest and closest friends, the late Marshall Field, who did so much for this university and for the cause of education in general, once said that he had known quite a few men who were considered to have been highly successful.

199

"I have known them well enough," he said, "to know that they suffer horribly from indigestion, from inability to assimilate what they have, and that they are wracked by regret for what success has cost them in loss of ideals, lack of identification with their fellowmen and remorse for the crushed souls and bodies left by the wayside."

What he was saying was, of course, that success—in this country at least—is all too frequently measured in terms of competitive acquisitiveness; and that the price paid for success measured in terms of wealth, power and privilege is often such as to destroy the happiness of its possessor.

That is why I have no formula for success and why I am not at all sure that I would wish you success, except insofar as its attainment may be consistent with your maintaining a good digestion, an untroubled conscience and a happy relationship with your fellow-men.

Secondly, I am not at all sure that anyone knows what for another person constitutes happiness. Many people do not even know the consistency of that happiness which they so eagerly seek for themselves. I know a great number of Americans in many walks of life and at all income levels for whom the pursuit of happiness apparently consists in nothing more than seeking to fill an ever-mounting shopping-list of material possessions. The pursuit of this kind of acquisitive satisfaction is unfortunately stimulated by a number of powerful pressure factors now present in the American society. The constant titillation of the acquisitive glands by a flood of advertising and by advertising-drenched entertainment is one such factor. The excessive expansion of installment credit is another. "Keeping up with the Joneses"—i.e. anxiety concerning social status—is a third. As a result of these and other pressures, many Americans go through life forever hocking their paychecks and forever increasing the mortgage upon their futures for the sake of new cars, new appliances and new gadgets most of which they consider disreputably out-of-date by the time they pay for them.

I do not wish you that kind of happiness. Insofar as I understand what happiness is—the kind of happiness that I hope you will achieve—I would say that it derives primarily from loving and being loved, from the satisfaction of work well done irrespective of reward or recognition, and that it derives only to a minor extent from the acquisition of possessions beyond those essential to a reasonably comfortable existence.

The third reason why I feel that it is inappropriate for me to offer you advice is because I belong to a generation which has, I think, disqualified itself as a source of wisdom. My generation inherited a world in which a student graduating from college could unconcernedly ask himself: "What shall I do with my future?" I am painfully aware that my generation has converted that relatively secure world into one in which you—and others like you all over the earth—must ask yourselves the much grimmer question: "*Is* there a future?"

The one extenuating circumstance which may perhaps justify my presence on this platform is that, for the greater part of my adult life, I have been an outspoken dissenter from many of those prevailing opinions and public policies which have contributed to creating the kind of world in which you will have to live.

As a dissenter from the generally smug attitude of the business community, to which I belonged as a banker in the Twenties and early Thirties, I was privileged to work for domestic reform under the great President for whom this university was named. As a dissenter from the aloof, ultra-nationalistic foreign policy at first pursued by that same President, I became for a time a New Deal renegade, returning to the fold only when our government showed signs of realizing that peace had become indivisible in a world from which the airplane had all but eliminated the elements of time and distance. Again working for our government during the war, I dissented fruitlessly from a policy which aimed at total victory and unconditional surrender, subordinating all political considerations to military expediency. Contrary to prevailing opinion, I did not believe that the wartime agreements with Russia could reasonably be expected to undo the harm done by the prewar appeasement of Hitler and by a subsequent conduct of the war which permitted the Soviet Union to intrude into Eastern Europe. I did not share the view that the San Francisco Conference of 1945 had created a world organization strong enough to preserve the peace, or that the Potsdam Agreement of the same year would result in the creation of a peaceful, democratic German nation. During the postwar years, I have, as a matter of fact, disagreed openly with almost every aspect of our foreign policy, except the Marshall Plan, the Point Four Program and the basic declaration of solidarity with Western Europe contained in the North Atlantic Treaty.

I disagree today with our government's inflexible and excessively military-minded policy in Europe, Africa and the Middle East.

This record of minority dissent does not absolve me from sharing the responsibility of my generation. Its sole relevance to this occasion is that these years of swimming upstream against the prevailing current of public opinion may perhaps have given me some slight insight into the problems which are your heritage.

Having said this, let me now try as best I can to answer the question, which is, I am sure, uppermost in your minds: Can you with reasonable assurance look forward to a future for yourselves and for the children you hope some day to raise? Or is it only a matter of time before our civilization will disintegrate in a final mushroom cloud of atomic particles?

My answer is as follows:

I firmly believe that there is a future—and not only that; I am convinced that the future you face is one in which the obvious dangers are dwarfed by almost unimaginable opportunities.

Admittedly, it is an act of faith to express such a belief. It is an act of faith to assert the conviction that man was not put upon this earth and endowed with reason by his Creator, merely in order that he should ultimately destroy himself in senseless, fratricidal conflict. This affirmation of confidence in man's survival implies, so far as I am concerned, more than a reliance upon the existence of a Divine purpose. It implies a belief in man's reason, in his sense of justice and in the innate preponderance in human nature of the creative, the cooperative and fraternal impulses, as against those drives which are competitively acquisitive, aggressive and ultimately suicidal. In other words, my belief that there *is* a future is not a belief that man *will* necessarily survive, no matter what he does. It is a conviction that man *can* survive if he makes proper use of the endowment given to him by his Maker.

Whether man does so survive depends not solely but to a very large extent upon the behavior of the American people in the years ahead. It is largely because I believe in the American people—which is to say in you and your generation—that I am able to profess the belief that there is a future.

I think I can now anticipate the question which next arises in your minds:

"How, in this strange new world, dominated by highly concentrated and secrecy-veiled power, can we, as ordinary citizens of the United States, participate in the shaping of human destiny?"

My answer would be, first of all, by *being* citizens of the United States; and, second, by being citizens of the world.

If you look around you at the young people who have recently graduated from college, you will find that most of them are essentially home-builders. Not knowing how they can contribute to a solution of the world's problems, they are making a bet that, somehow, there will be a future for them and for their children. These young people are for the most part hard-working, either married or looking forward to marriage, and, when married, usually devoted husbands, wives and parents. Beyond being home-builders, they work on PTAs and on hospital and community chest committees. Often, they take an intelligent interest in local politics. Yet all these activities, admirable as they are, add up to a concentration upon private community life and to a withdrawal from participation in the affairs of the nation and the world.

The people who live in this manner are making a brave bet upon the future, but they are doing little, either as American citizens or as citizens of the world, to make their hopes come true.

Again, if you look around, you will find other people who are not making any brave bets upon the future and who, because they doubt whether there is a future, are inclined to "eat, drink and be merry" while they can. These men and women tend to remain single or, if they marry, they hesitate to bring children into the world. They are doing even less to assure the existence of a future than the home-builders.

Neither of these two attitudes is caused by a lack of interest and certainly neither is caused by the absence of anxiety. Both are primarily due, I think, to a sense of frustration—to a feeling that there is actually nothing an individual can do to affect the course of history.

Far more than I wish you success in whatever careers you may choose to enter, I wish you emancipation from this sense of helplessness and frustration. If it were in my power to bestow upon each and every one of you a single gift, it would be the realization that the really important decisions are essentially simple, though often involving a difficult choice of alternatives; and that the making of these decisions does not lie beyond the reach of your influence.

Most of the mistakes we make as a nation do not arise from a wrong choice of alternatives but from failure to make a choice between alternative courses of action. This is partly because popularly elected leaders are usually reluctant to risk their popularity by so much as suggesting that there is a price-tag on every objective of national policy. The result is all too often a have-your-cake-and-eat-it policy which satisfies neither the appetite nor the desire to maintain a full larder. In national policy, even more than in private life, you cannot get something for nothing.

The advice which I offer you in this respect is simple. If you want your country to pursue a certain objective, like, for instance, universal disarmament, find out what it costs. Find out that there can be no reliably enforced disarmament without world law and a policeman empowered to enforce it. Find out that to establish world law and an enforcement agency superior to the national governments, certain sacrifices of national sovereignty are necessary. Then make up your mind whether you want universal national disarmament enough so that you are willing to pay the price, or else decide that, rather than sacrifice any part of national sovereignty, you prefer to continue living in a precarious peace preserved by a balance of terror.

Having reached your decision, the next step is to join whatever pressure group already exists for the purpose of furthering disarmament, if you are for it; or for the purpose of opposing it, if you are against it. By doing so, you will learn the arguments which have already been developed in favor of the course of which you think you approve. This may either strengthen your conviction or cause you to re-examine your position. In either case, you will have acquired an informed opinion. In either case, you will have discovered that, by ganging up with others, you actually have power.

Contrary to what many people think, there is nothing inherently reprehensible about pressure groups. Like every other political device, they can be misused; but there is no reason why farmers should not unite in order to obtain a hearing for their views on price supports or why labor should not unite to fight for or against legislation affecting its interest, or why any group of citizens having a common interest should not band together in order to further it. Indeed, there is scarcely any other way for the individual citizen to make him or herself effective in a mass society such as ours.

Belonging to one or more pressure groups will also make you better able to judge which candidates for office in an election year seem most likely to further the policies in which you believe.

The only other advice I can give you in this connection is to devote a certain part of each day, no matter how busy you may be, to keeping yourself informed about the developments in the nation and in a rapidly changing world. The first thing I do every morning is to read and clip the *New York Times*. A regularly read daily newspaper—provided that it is a good newspaper—is, I think, vastly more useful than trying to catch up once a week by reading the boiled-down and not wholly rounded reports of weekly news magazines. In addition to getting the facts, it is important to be familiar with current opinion generated by events. I would urge you to read or listen to not only the columnists, editorial writers and commentators with whom you generally agree but also those with whom you wholly disagree. Contrary opinion is the whetstone upon which to sharpen your convictions.

Another way to keep informed is to join the nearest World Affairs Council, Foreign Policy Association or other study group, to participate in its activities and to subscribe to its pamphlets and bulletins. The latter will often suggest supplementary reading on subjects in which you happen to be particularly interested. Here I should like to offer a technical suggestion.

Learn to skim-read. Few writers of books on contemporary subjects—and I say this as one of them—deserve more than an eclectic perusal of what they have to say. By skim-reading I do not, of course, mean careless reading. On the contrary, intelligent skim-reading requires a high degree of concentration, the ability to absorb the sense rather than the words and the capacity to weed out what is unimportant for your purposes.

It may seem to some of you that I am prescribing a rather heavy chore. Indeed, I am. I am suggesting that you owe it to yourselves to continue your education from now until the day you die. Yet I venture to express the belief that most of you will not consider this task too burdensome; that most of you are, in fact, eager for assignments; and that what you resent most is the absence of any demand upon your intelligence and your capacity for constructive effort.

If this supposition is correct, there is one thing I can promise you: once you acquire the self-disciplined habit of keeping yourselves informed, you will enjoy the effort more than you enjoy most entertainment. There are few things more fascinating than acquiring, exchanging and sharing new knowledge. There are few things more satisfactory than putting newly acquired knowledge to creative use.

The right of free inquiry, the right of free discussion and the right to dissent from prevailing majority opinion are among the most precious rights of citizens in a free society. I hope you will use them to the full, bearing in mind the wise words of William the Silent:

"It is not necessary to succeed in order to make the effort worth while."

So much for becoming responsible citizens of the United States. Let me now speak very briefly about becoming responsible citizens of the world.

Some years ago, Stringfellow Barr, the former president of St. John's College, wrote a pamphlet entitled: *"Let's Join the Human Race."* This title has embedded itself in my mind as the most succinct formulation of one of the major imperatives for the survival of Western man.

The time has passed when that small minority of the human race which inhabits the North Atlantic Basin can expect to live in relative abundance and security while the rest of humanity suffers hunger and privation. The time has passed when this small Atlantic minority, predominantly white-skinned, can expect to dominate the predominantly non-white majority of mankind. Either we join the human race or else we shall be rejected and submerged by its majority.

It is in this field that truly challenging opportunities stretch out before you. Some of these opportunities lie here at home; others lie abroad. The elimination of race prejudice here at home is a sphere of activity in which every one of you can participate. It is not necessary for me to emphasize this point to graduates of Roosevelt University. I doubt, however, whether many of you have had an opportunity to see at first hand how tragically the prestige of the United States suffers in Asia, Africa and the Middle East because we have failed as yet to establish full first-class citizenship for the American Negro. This is not just a domestic problem. It is a vitally important factor in the relations of the United States to the rest of the world. So long as this albatross hangs around our necks, there is not the slightest chance that we shall win the friendship of the Asian and African peoples.

Granted that our domestic race relations are bad enough, they appear infinitely worse than they actually are to people who have had no opportunity to observe the slow but steady progress that is being made. This is where I think you could do an infinite amount of good. I have in mind, for example, the possibility that inter-racial groups of Roosevelt graduates might organize visits to such countries as India, Burma, Indonesia or Ghana; that other such groups might go to work or study in Asian or African countries; and that return visits to Roosevelt University might be encouraged and financed on a scholarship basis. I can think of no better ambassadors to these vitally important parts of the world than graduates of this university. I can think of no enterprise more worthy of the support of the older generations of Americans.

Whether or not these specific suggestions appeal to you, I should like to leave with you the thought that the best insurance against war is increasing intercourse among the world's peoples. The more we of the West learn the languages, the history and the cultures of the non-Western peoples, and the more familiar the non-Western peoples become with us at first hand, the less will be the chance of misunderstanding. Whatever you can do in this direction will be a contribution to the firm establishment of peace, whether you do your bit as students or as teachers, as business representatives or as emissaries of our government, as newspaper reporters or as doctors and nurses. The relationship of peoples to peoples is infinitely more important than the relationship of governments to governments.

Finally, I should like to say in all honesty that I envy you. In spite of the uncertainties that overhang your future, the beginning of your adult life coincides with the beginning of a revolutionary new age of man. You are not encumbered by the emotional and intellectual baggage of an age that is past. You carry no burden of responsibility for past error. You are not the prisoners of old commitments which have now become irrelevant. You are free to meet the challenge of a new age with open eyes, open minds and open hearts. You are free to break new ground as no Americans have been free since the days of our pioneering ancestors. Before them lay an unexplored continent. Before you lies an unexplored world.

And so I wish you not snug security but a life full of adventure—a life in which you will not avoid danger but meet it unafraid—a life upon which some day you may look back with a sense of work well done, not just for yourselves and your families—and not just for your country, but for your fellow man.